KAREN COMMINGS

The Cat Lover's Survival Guide:

Helpful Hints for Solving Your Most Pesky Pet Problems

D1529879

BARRON'S

ACKNOWLEDGMENTS

I would like to express my sincere thanks to these people, who provided me with information, tips, and suggestions: Donna Allen, Fenda Alp (American Pet Products Manufacturers Association), Allan Arthur, Carol Banks, Jackie Burgen, Jane Buxton and Morgan the guide dog, Barb Eichorn, Judy Heim, Dana R. Miller, Mary Osterberg, Catherine S. Perel, Bonnie Rayho, Erica Marie Stark, Eileen A. Stone, and Steve Wayland (program director, PAWS/LA).

•••

All inquiries should be addressed to:
Barron's Educational Series, Inc.
250 Wireless Boulevard
Hauppauge, NY 11788
http://www.barronseduc.com

International Standard Book No. 0-7641-1576-6
Library of Congress Catalog Card No. 00-059890

Library of Congress Cataloging-in-Publication Data
Commings, Karen.
 The cat lover's survival guide : helpful hints for solving your most
 pesky pet problems / Karen Commings.
  p. cm.
 ISBN 0-7641-1576-6
 1. Cats. I. Title.
SF447.C64 2001
636.8'088'7—dc21   00-059890

Printed in the United States of America
9 8 7 6 5 4 3 2 1

Contents

Behavior Tips / 62

Seasonal Tips / 82

Helpful Hints for Cats with Disabilities / 101

Helpful Hints for Cat Owners with Disabilities / 111

Pet Supply Sources / 122

Index / 124

Introduction

As anyone who has made a career of adopting cats will tell you, there are successes and there are occasional failures. My failure came in the form of three two-year-old, feline littermates who were surrendered to a shelter after their elderly owner had died. The deceased cat owner willed money to the shelter with the stipulation that the three male cats, Leo, Luke, and Tony, be placed together into one home. The cats were so wonderful I decided to adopt them. Since I knew that they should be introduced to my four cats one at a time, I decided to confine them temporarily to an unused bedroom on my second floor. This would have worked except for one tiny problem. Within seconds of placing their dishes of food onto the floor, the food was covered with ants. Like tiny soldiers absorbed in the objectives of battle, the ants appeared out of nowhere, marched single file across the room to the cats' food dishes, and carried off the contents, leaving the three cats looking bewildered and confused.

I had no ants anywhere else in the house, but that room was the only one in which I could keep the three brothers until I gradually introduced them to my other cats. Not wanting the cats to eat ant-ridden food forced me to allow them immediate access to the rest of the house. As a result, they immediately comingled with my four resident cats. The relationship was never successful because the three newcomers, who were very close, teamed up against my other four cats, who were also very close. After three months of trying to make the situation work, I had to admit defeat and took the three brothers back to the shelter to be placed into another home. Because the shelter was no-kill, I was comforted somewhat by the fact that the cats would stay there until someone adopted them.

What does this story have to do with a household hint? I have since learned that setting a bowl of pet food inside a larger saucer filled with water will prevent ants from attacking the food. Ants do not swim and will not cross the water to get to the food. In fact, so simple is the trick that a pet food bowl is now on the market with an attached saucer underneath for water. Had I known this ten years ago when I temporarily confined Leo, Luke, and Tony, I would still have them to this day. I think of them often and wish with all my heart that I had been able to prevent a small problem from developing into a bigger one, forcing me to ask the shelter to place the cats elsewhere. As a result of this painful episode, I learned that just a simple household hint can help a pet owner make the situation work when everything else fails. It is my hope that in this book, you will be able to find answers to some of your more perplexing cat-related problems and, by doing so, will help ensure that your experience with your cat companion is a rewarding one.

Cleaning Tips

Unlike the joy and comfort of listening to a cat purr or the thrill of observing a cat's enthusiasm as she chases a crumpled paper ball, cleaning is one of those tasks for which the primary reward is getting it over with so we can go on to something else more enjoyable. Teaching a kitten to use the litter box goes a long way in reducing the amount of time you will spend cleaning up your cat's accidents. For additional help cutting down the cleanup time, try some of the ideas in this chapter.

Cleanliness Is Next To . . .

Perhaps Fluffy had an accident while waiting for you to come home from the office and clean the box. Instead, maybe Fluffy occasionally coughs up a hair ball that includes some of the food she had for dinner. The following lists some ways to keep periodic accidents from becoming permanent memories.

• Pre-mix in spray bottles appropriate cleaning products, such as vinegar and water or detergent and water, so the products are handy when you need them. Label the spray bottles with their contents, and store them in a convenient location. Often, just spraying the cleaning products onto the spot where Fluffy upchucked her dinner will help lift up the residue and prevent stains from forming.

• Manufacturers have marked their upholstered furniture with a cleaning code or set of instructions to let the consumer know what type of cleaning is recommended for that product. The codes are usually on the furniture platforms under the cushions. A W, for example, means that the product should be cleaned

with only water, while the letter *S* means the furniture should be cleaned with only solvents. Before using any cleaning product on your upholstered furniture, check the manufacturer's instructions, and test clean a spot in an inconspicuous place.

• Treat your carpet and upholstered furniture with a stain-resistant product such as SCOTCHGARD.

If your cat upchucks a hair ball

• Allow the hair ball to dry. Rubbing the soiled spot while still wet makes a bigger mess. Place a dish over the spot to keep from stepping into it. When dry, lift up the hair ball, and scrape any residue up with a fork. Vacuum the spot to remove any remaining particles. Clean the area with an enzyme cleaner, a three-to-one

HOW-TO: Remove Urine from Carpet

Most carpet manufacturers print care instructions for the carpet they produce. If you have an older carpet or do not know the name of your carpet's manufacturer, follow these easy steps to remove urine when your pet has an accident. **A word of caution: Never use ammonia on a urine spot. Urine is ammonia based and will entice your cat to return to the spot to urinate.** *If you can smell telltale urine in your carpet but can't find it, use a black light to pinpoint the spots to make cleaning the carpet easier.*

1. *Blot up the urine as quickly as possible with a dry cloth or paper towel.*
2. *Apply a small amount of diluted detergent solution consisting of 1/4 teaspoon (1.2 ml) mild liquid dishwashing detergent and 1 quart (1 L) water, or use a solution of 1/4 cup (60 ml) vinegar and 1 quart (1 L) water.*
3. *Press the solution into the urine spot, and continue to blot up the excess. Do not rub the urine into the carpet.*
4. *Rinse the spot with clear water or an odor neutralizer and blot dry.*
5. *Place paper towels or clean, dry cleaning cloths over the area, and weight them down. Change the paper towels or cloths as soon as they have become saturated with liquid, and apply dry ones. Continue this process until the carpet is dry.*
6. *After the spot has dried, brush up the piling and vacuum the area. Be sure the spot is completely dry before walking on it.*

vinegar-and-water mixture, or a stain remover. You can also follow the steps for removing vomit as listed below.

• An alternative is to sprinkle baking soda onto the hair ball and allow it to absorb the liquid if the hair ball is recent and still wet. Scoop up the mess with a paper towel, and follow with an effective spot remover or club soda.

Where your cat enjoys rubbing

• If your cat enjoys rubbing her face on corners, clean the corners by using cleanser or baking soda on a damp sponge. If your walls are papered, use a little isopropyl alcohol or baking soda on a damp sponge. If your walls are paneled, mix one part vinegar to two parts water, clean with a damp sponge, wipe dry, then follow with a wood polish.

HOW-TO: Remove Vomit from Carpet

Cats may vomit because they may have eaten too fast, they may be warm, or they may be stressed. If your cat vomits more than three times in a six-hour period, have her examined by a veterinarian. If you are faced with removing vomit from carpet, follow the steps below. Food with added dyes can discolor fabric or carpet if your cat vomits her dinner, so clean up the deposit as quickly as possible.

1. *Use a spoon or fork to remove solid or dried materials from the vomit.*
2. *If the stain is large, work from the outside to the center to prevent it from spreading. Blot up any liquid with a paper towel or cloth.*
3. *Apply a solution of 1 teaspoon (5 ml) detergent and 1 quart (1 L) water to the area, then dampen the area with a cloth. Don't rub the stain into the carpet or use a brush while the carpet is wet because you might damage the carpet fibers.*
4. *If necessary, put on some rubber gloves and work the detergent solution into the carpet.*
5. *Wet the carpet with clear water to rinse.*
6. *Place clean paper towels or cleaning cloths onto the area, and weight them down. Change the paper towels when they have absorbed liquid.*
7. *After the spot has dried, brush up the piling and vacuum the area. Be sure the spot is completely dry before walking on it.*

• Mount a comber onto the corner of the wall. Your cat can rub her face and whiskers onto the comber without leaving dirty deposits. Corner combers are available in pet stores.

Germ Warfare

Humans will probably catch more harmful germs from other people or even the food we eat than from animals. However, eliminating bacteria from surfaces on which our cats walk can help make our homes more sanitary. Here are some weapons for your war against germs.

• Use common, household bleach or other less caustic disinfectants to eliminate harmful bacteria. Rinse well, and do not allow your cat to walk on the surface while it's wet. If the bleach gets onto your cat's paws, she can ingest it when she licks her feet. *Caution: Pretest a surface before cleaning with bleach to avoid color changes.*

• Instead, use an antibacterial cleaner with an odor neutralizer to remove bacteria and leave your house clean smelling.

After scooping the litter box, use an antibacterial soap to wash your hands.

• Wash cat food dishes with detergent at least once a week to prevent bacterial growth. If your cat's food and water bowls are dishwasher safe, place them in the dishwasher, where the high temperature will kill bacteria.

• Use an antibacterial litter to prevent the spread of germs on your cat's paws when she leaves the litter box.

Hair and There

Do you arrive at the office looking like you were attacked by a large furball? Do your dinner guests politely pick pet hair from their food before eating it? Nothing says "I have a cat" more than hair clinging to our clothing, hair wafting through the air in our homes, or hair burrowing into the butter. Frequent vacuuming is one of the best ways to cut down on hair buildup. However, if you don't always have time to cart out the vacuum cleaner, try some of these suggestions for cleaning up the piles of pet hair.

• To sweep up loose pet hair from hardwood or vinyl floors, use a dampened mop or a mop with a disposable, treated cloth.

• Wall-to-wall carpet holds down the hair more than hardwood or vinyl floors, so adding carpet to a room may help keep cat hair from wafting through your house.

• To pick up loose cat hair attached to upholstered furniture, wear a dampened rubber glove or use a dampened sponge.

• Use a washable, recyclable sticky roller to lift cat hair from fabrics and upholstery.

• Purchase a washable pet hair remover to help you wipe off cat hair from clothing, furniture, or pillows. Place it under your furniture cushions for easy access.

• To pick up cat hair from your carpet, use a window squeegee.

• Choose furniture made from smooth fabrics such as leather, faux leather, satin, or other fabric to which loose hair will not stick as readily.

• Place a washable towel or blanket over your cat's favorite sleeping spot to keep hair from clinging to cushions.

• Use washable window coverings if your cat likes to watch the world go by from a window seat or on the floor in front of a picture window or patio doors.

• Drapes made of smooth fabrics will not attract as much hair as heavy, textured drapes. If you're in the market for some new window furnishings, purchase ones that are less likely to become laden with your cat's hair.

• Tie-back curtains will keep your cat from depositing hair onto them if she likes to sit in the window.

• Keep a lint brush near your favorite easy chair. After your cat sits on your lap, you can roll off the cat hair before you get up.

• Use a feather duster or device to clean between slats of mini-blinds to remove deposited hair.

• Change the furnace and air conditioner filters more often during shedding season to prevent blockage.

• Use a hard-bristled hair brush to brush up the cat hair on carpeted cat trees.

Hair on clothes

• Keep a roll of masking tape or a sticky roller in your car to remove cat hair after you leave the house. Keep some in your office drawer at work to do the same.

• Remove cat hair from your clothing with a dampened rubber glove, sticky roller, or masking tape or blow it off with a blow-dryer.

Hair on bedding

• Run your bedding through the air-dry or fluff cycle of your dryer to remove hair before putting it in the washing machine.

• If some cat hair remains at the bottom of the washing machine after you have done your laundry, remove the hair by running the washer through one rinse cycle.

Hair in drains

- If your cat's hair accompanies you into the shower and clogs the drain or your drains run slowly after giving your cat a bath in the sink or tub, keep a plunger handy. Hand plungers come in many sizes for different-sized drains. Some have short handles for unclogging a sink, and others have longer handles to reach the drains in a tub or shower. Plunge after each use to keep the cat hair from severely clogging your drains.

- Purchase a mechanical plunger for those hairy pipes. All types of plungers are available in hardware stores and builders' supply outlets.

- Place some steel wool into your drain to trap hair.

Managing the Pet Poop

Even though we don't like to think about it, waste management goes with the territory in cat ownership. Keeping Kitty's box clean is a way to ensure that she keeps using it and family members and guests do not smell it as soon as they arrive. If piles of pet poop get you down, try some of these suggestions to keep from being overwhelmed by your cat's wastes.

- Feed your cat a highly digestible, high-quality food to reduce the volume of her stools.

- After a kitty constitutional, your cat will inevitably have bits and pieces of litter stuck to her feet when she leaves the litter box regardless of the type of litter you use. Place a sisal or green, turf-style mat in front of the box to trap the pieces of litter. Periodically, shake out the mat.

- Purchase from a pet store a plastic mat designed to trap bits of litter as your cat exits the box. The molded plastic mat fits snugly under the litter box.

- To keep litter from sticking to the bottom of the litter box, spray the box with a vegetable cooking spray.

- If you use scooping litter, put wastes into a plastic, zipper-style food bag to prevent odor buildup in your trash can.

- Use a litter scoop with a hole in the back of the handle to which you attach a plastic bag that enables you to scoop and toss the litter at the same time. Such devices are available in pet stores.

- If scooping the box is one of your least-favorite activities, purchase a self-cleaning cat box that cleans itself every time your cat makes a deposit. This will automatically rake the waste into disposable containers ten minutes after your cat steps out of the box. *Important: Because illnesses often show up first in your cat's wastes, be sure to check your cat's wastes daily to make sure that your cat does not have diarrhea, is not constipated, and is urinating appropriately.*

- If carrying bags of Fluffy's wastes to the trash doesn't turn you on, try a flushable litter that you can scoop into the toilet.

- If keeping Fido from inserting his nose or the kids from inserting their hands into your cat's litter box is a constant battle, purchase a covered litter box with a retractable hood and a security button latch that prevents anyone or anything but your cat from entering the box.

- If you don't like the litter box taking up so much space, buy a triangular, covered box that fits into a corner. The box includes a handled screen to scoop and dispose of wastes in one fell swoop.

- Litter liners help keep kitty wastes from soaking into the litter box and can be removed for easy disposal. If your cat scratches the liner, place layers of newspaper on top of the liner before putting litter into the box.

- To dispose of litter that is not flushable, place the used litter in plastic-handled grocery bags, tie them up, and place them at the curb.

- If you use clay litter, line your litter box with cardboard flats in which cases of soda, beer, or cat food are sold. Every few days, simply lift out the box and dispose of it and the dirty litter.

- Strain your clumping litter occasionally with a colander to remove smaller pieces of feces. Do not use the colander in the kitchen after it has been through the litter box.

- Litter box alternatives include recycle bins and plastic cement mixing tubs available at hardware stores. Cut a U-shaped opening in one end for your cat to enter.

- If your home is a small apartment and potential litter box locations are at a minimum, investigate purchasing a litter box that looks like a piece of furniture or ones that look like planters-complete with silk foliage. Such boxes are attractive and fit in with a variety of decors. Check the classifieds in the backs of the major cat magazines for vendors.

- Attach a stick-on odor repellent to the back or side of your cat's litter box to help reduce odors.

- If your cat raises its rear while urinating in the box, layer newspaper under the box and stagger the sections out from the box so that the soiled paper can be rolled up, leaving extra layers underneath to catch the overflow.

- Finally, if you're up for the challenge, toilet train Kitty to use your facilities rather than providing your cat with her own. Specially designed litter boxes are available to toilet train cats.

The Nose Knows

No matter how often our cats wash themselves or we wash them, sometimes, just having a cat in the house can leave a telltale smell. Long after the stain is lifted, odors can linger. Follow some of these suggestions to keep from being entrenched in stench.

Pee-u!

• Odors and stains from feces or urine are protein based and require an odor neutralizer containing bacterial enzymes to eliminate them completely. Purchase enzyme products at discount department stores, health food stores, or pet stores. If you attend cat shows, you may find vendors who sell odor neutralizers intended to eliminate pet odors. Odor neutralizers may be added to the laundry to remove odors from bedding and leave it clean smelling.

• Purchase an electronic air-cleaning system designed to remove pet odors from the air as well as cold and flu viruses.

• Make your own carpet freshener by combining one box of baking soda with 1 tablespoon (15 ml) of orrisroot (available in herb stores) that has been saturated in your favorite scented oil. Place the mixture into a glass jar, and cover with a metal lid in which you have punched holes. Let it sit for a few days so that the baking soda picks up the oil scent. Then sprinkle it onto the carpet before vacuuming. The jar lid will prevent the orrisroot from spilling out, so you can reuse it by just adding more baking soda. Sprinkle the mixture onto the carpet, let it sit for 15 or 20 minutes, then vacuum.

• Use a window fan set on exhaust to make odor elimination a breeze.

Litter box blues

• One of the primary sources of odor in a household with cats is the litter box. To cut down on litter box odor, use scented litter. If your cat objects to a perfume-smelling litter box, sprinkle some baking soda into your cat's box instead.

- Clean the litter box monthly with sudsy water. Then follow with a vinegar rinse or odor neutralizer.

- Try a covered litter box with a charcoal filter in the top, which helps trap and eliminate litter box odor.

- Plastic litter boxes tend to retain odors. As an alternative, try a box made from stainless steel or other materials that do not absorb odor. If you cannot find a stainless steel box, try a basin from a restaurant supply store.

- To keep litter box odors from building up in your home altogether, investigate the option of one in which indoor cats enter via a pet door in the wall of your home. The covered box attaches to the wall and is completely safe for your cat to enter without fear of her escaping your house.

- To help fight litter box odor, try a cedar chip litter. *Caution: Cedar chip litter can irritate the mucous membranes of some cats.*

Post-Meal Cleanup

Unless you are cooking your cat's meals instead of serving them from a bag, box, or can, after-meal cleanup should not be complicated. Let's face it, though, some cats, like some people, are just sloppy eaters. Instead of trying to improve your cat's mealtime manners, try some of these suggestions.

- Coat your cat's food bowls with vegetable cooking spray to keep food from sticking to them.

- Purchase non-stick bowls for your cat. Non-stick bowls are available in kitchen stores or housewares departments.

- To keep food from flying onto the floor around your cat's food dish, place the dish on a tray instead of a place mat.

- Use a coffee filter as a food bowl which can be thrown away after use.

• Plastic salad bar containers with lid and bottom still connected can become food and water dishes or a tray on which to sit your cat's regular bowl to keep food and water from spilling. They are also a good way to feed two cats at once and recycle those plastic containers at the same time.

• If you are caring for a litter of kittens that have been weaned, feed them from a muffin tin to keep cleanup chores to a minimum.

Smudges and Streaks

Does your cat enjoy watching the world go by from the windows or glass patio doors? If so, you may have smudges and streaks from your cat pressing her nose against the glass to get a better view. Keeping your cat away from windows and doors deprives her of one of the supreme pleasures of an indoor pet. However, if you want to keep up with eliminating smudges and streaks on your windows and doors, follow some of these suggestions.

• To keep smudge cleanup to a minimum, compromise with your cat and designate one or two locations as lookout spots. Place objects or nonpoisonous plants onto the other windowsills so that your cat cannot access them.

• In a spray bottle, mix one part vinegar to three parts water as a glass cleaner and keep it handy. Clean with a lint-free cloth or squeegee dry.

• To prevent your cat from smudging glass in doors, choose gathered curtains that are held down by a curtain rod at the top and bottom so that she cannot get her nose to the glass.

Cleaning Resources

For information about toilet training your cat, check out this title:

 Kunkel, Paul, "How to Toilet Train Your Cat: 21 Days to a Litter-Free Home," New York: Workman Publishing Company, 1991.

Cost-Saving Tips

Americans spend more than 21 billion dollars annually on pet food, products, services, and veterinary care. At times, you probably feel like a large portion of that is coming from your wallet. Although you will not want to skimp on your cat's health or nutritional needs, you can save money on her care in some ways. Whether you have one cat or a dozen, the following techniques will help your cat care dollar stretch a little further.

General Cost-Saving Tips

• One of the nice features of cat shows—besides seeing so many beautiful animals—is the plethora of vendors who set up shop to sell their wares to those who enter and attend the show. The products are often cheaper than the same or similar products you can find in a pet store. So, relax, enjoy the show, and stock up on pet supplies to save some money.

• Clip and use store coupons on food and related pet items. If you have more coupons than you can use, place extras into the pet aisles of your grocery store or donate them to a local shelter or animal organization.

• Watch ads in your local newspapers for sales at local pet stores and pet warehouses. You may find buy-one-and-get-one free promotions or even obtain premium food and products at minimal costs.

• Buy food, cat litter, and other items in larger sizes, which are cheaper per ounce (gram).

- Shop at yard sales and flea markets to find items that your cat can use. You may be lucky enough to find inexpensive carriers, beds, bowls, toys, and other items you will need for her.

- Take advantage of manufacturers' promotional sales. These often come with added pet products for minimal costs. Although some promotions require you to send away for the products, the cost of postage is far less than the cost of the product if you had to buy it.

- If you have Internet access, shop for pet supplies on-line. You may find what you need at less cost than in a pet store.

Bedding Down

Go into any pet store or shop in any pet supply catalog, and you'll find cat beds in a myriad of styles to match any decor. Although lovely, pet beds can be pretty pricey, leaving one to wonder why we would want to spend so much money on something our cats use with their eyes closed. The cheapest way to provide your cat with a bed is to let her share yours. However, if you'd like your cat to have her own sleeping quarters at a lower cost than those you find at retail prices, here are some ideas.

- Shop at flea markets for old, wooden shipping crates. Line them with blankets for a comfy sleeping spot.

- Purchase beds that have washable covers to prevent replacing the beds as often.

- At flea markets and yard sales, buy old quilts or blankets for your cat's bedding.

- Save those old towels and blankets for your cat to sleep on.

- Fill an old pillowcase with a soft piece of foam rubber. Sew the end shut. You will have a comfortable, washable bed, and your cat will appreciate having a bed made from something that is yours.

• Purchase a pillow that has a smaller pillow attached for your cat to sleep on. You will save money and have a more comfortable night's sleep at the same time.

Cleaning Up

Cleaning is generally more time-consuming than costly, but commercial cleaning products can cost an arm and a leg. If you would like to eliminate the expense of cleaning up after your cat, try some of these low-cost alternatives to dealing with cat messes.

• Baking soda makes an excellent, cheap alternative to cleaning those kitty rub marks from the corners of your walls. It also can be used in your cat's litter box or as a dry shampoo.

• If you bathe your cat in a sink or bathtub, hair can build up and clog the drain. For less than the price of one container of drain cleaner, you can purchase a hand plunger to remove clogged cat hair from your pipes.

HOW-TO: Make a T-shirt Cat Bed

A bed made from one of your old t-shirts will be especially appealing to your cat. Making your cat a t-shirt bed will be emotionally rewarding and save you money at the same time. The t-shirt bed can be machine washed and dried when it becomes dirty.

1. *Sew the armholes and neck hole of the shirt closed.*
2. *Fill the top half of the shirt with whatever washable stuffing you choose.*
3. *Sew a seam across the mid-section of the shirt just below the arms to trap the stuffing in the top half.*
4. *Sew another seam from the center of the mid-section seam to the bottom of the shirt, creating two sections in the lower half of the t-shirt.*
5. *Stuff both sections, then sew the bottom shut.*
6. *Fold over the sleeves, and hand stitch them to the underside of the bed.*

You have created a bed with three pillowed sections. Place the bed anywhere your cat likes to sleep. Your cat will love you for making it.

• Add some white vinegar to the rinse water when you wash your cat's bedding to remove odors, or rinse your cat with one part vinegar to four parts water after a bath.

Food and Water Bowls

Cats do not care what their food and water bowls look like—only what's in them. Pet food bowls are designed for the owner rather than the pet. Your cat will love you just as much if you provide her nourishment in an old pie plate as she will if you offer food in a specially made cat food bowl. Instead of spending money on something that will not make a difference in your cat's well-being, try one of these low-cost solutions to pet platters.

• Place your cat's food in a plastic food storage container. When your cat is finished chowing down, put the lid on and place the uneaten portion of food in the refrigerator to keep it fresh.

• If your cat eats dry and canned food, serve it on a divided plate such as those used for picnics instead of providing two bowls.

• Place your cat's food bowls on an old, rubber dish drainer to prevent spills and keep bits and pieces of food from falling onto the floor.

• Another idea for a pet place mat is to use the shallow cardboard cartons in which cases of pet food are sold. For extra protection for your floors, leave the plastic covering on the cardboard case before placing your cat's food and water bowls on it.

• If your cat leaves some of her canned food in her bowl to snack on later, cover the dish with a lightweight plastic container, such as those in which cottage cheese come, to keep the food from drying out. Your cat should be able to knock the lid off to get to the food when she is hungry. If your cat has trouble with the concept, show her how to remove the cover until she learns the technique.

- Instead of bowls, use heavy glass ashtrays available at dollar stores. The weight prevents them from sliding around the floor.

- Visit flea markets and yard sales to find inexpensive saucers and bowls to use for your cat's food.

Health Care Solutions

Your cat deserves the best veterinary care to help her live a long and happy life. Providing your pet with annual checkups, vaccinations, and medical care when she needs it is one way to ensure that the two of you spend many years together. However, you can reduce the costs of basic health care in some ways.

- If you adopted your cat from a shelter, your cat might have received the important spay or neuter surgery before being placed. If you adopted a purebred cat from a breeder, the breeder may have spayed or neutered the cat prior to sale. If your cat has not been altered, contact a local shelter, animal organization, or your veterinarian to determine if low-cost spaying and neutering are available. If you cannot find a local group, contact SPAY USA, a network of volunteers and veterinarians working together to popularize and facilitate spay/neuter services through a nationwide toll-free referral service.

- Larger shelters may operate veterinary clinics to serve the needs of the animals that are surrendered to them. In some cases, the shelter-run clinics are open to the public and may offer veterinary services at a lower cost than veterinarians in private practice. Contact the shelters in your area to see if they offer veterinary services.

- States in which rabies is more prevalent may require that you obtain an annual rabies shot for your cat. Local shelters and animal organizations may offer rabies shots by their own veterinarians at a lower cost than your veterinarian might. Contact the shelters in your area to determine if they have a low-cost rabies vaccination program.

• If you have more than one cat, ask your veterinarian if he or she offers multi-pet discounts. Many veterinarians offer a savings to cat owners on visits for two or more cats.

• Discuss with your veterinarian pet health insurance options that may help you save money on veterinary care.

• If you are planning to adopt two cats at the same time from a shelter, ask if the shelter offers a discount on the second cat. Many shelters will reduce the cost for adoption when a prospective pet parent wants more than one animal at time.

Pet Playthings

When it comes to play, cats just wanna' have fun. Your cat will enjoy the workout as much or more than the toy when you involve her in a favorite game. Commercially available toys are wonderful, but they can be expensive. To provide your cat with inexpensive playthings, try some of these low-cost or no-cost alternatives.

• Visit flea markets and yard sales to find old children's stuffed toys that can be used as cat toys. Very often, these toys have been cleaned and are ready for the next owner. Cats will enjoy wrapping their paws around and kicking them. To add some interest for your cat, partially cut a seam and insert some catnip, then sew it back up for a great cat toy. *Caution: Be sure to remove from the toys any small parts such as beaded eyes so that your cat doesn't accidentally swallow them.*

• Let your cat chase the light from a flashlight as you shine it up a wall or over the floor.

• Hide your cat's toys around the house. Finding them will give her something to do when you are not at home, and rotating the toys will keep her interested in her playthings.

• Your cat will love to chase a stretchable, spiral shoelace as long as you are at the other end. *Caution: When finished playing, be sure to put the shoelace away so your cat doesn't decide to chew and swallow it.*

• Fill old medicine bottles with dried corn or beans, and roll them on the floor for your cat to chase.

• Use those old shoulder pads you've removed from garments to make a shoulder pad catnip mouse. Fold the shoulder pad in half, and stitch up the curved side using an overhand stitch and a contrasting color of thread. Sprinkle catnip into the open end, then stitch it up using the same overhand stitch. To make the toy more attractive, sew some whiskers onto the pointed end, or embroider two eyes to make the toy look more like a mouse.

• Roll a table tennis ball or plastic, practice golf ball in the bathtub for your cat to chase.

• Make your cat an interactive toy that she can use on her own by recycling those old shoe boxes. Cut holes into the sides and top of the box big enough for your cat to stick her paw into. Place an old table tennis ball inside. Secure the lid with some masking tape. Place it onto the floor for your cat to reach inside to bat the ball.

• Put those catnip toys that have lost their novelty into a container of loose catnip to regain their odor and make them appealing again.

• Crumple paper into a wad for your cat to chase.

• Place a paper, handle-free grocery sack on the floor for your cat to slide in and out of.

• Cut sponges into 3-inch (8-cm) squares, and hide them around the house.

- Cut openings into a large, cardboard box.

- Place a rubber ball into an open egg carton. Show your cat how to bat the ball from one section to another.

- Cut off the cuff of a sock slightly above the ankle. Stuff the cuff into the toe of the sock. Sprinkle some loose catnip into the sock. Stretch the open end, and tie it into an overhand knot. If you like, embroider a face onto the front of the sock to make it look a little fancier.

Pet Poop

Wouldn't you rather spend your money on what goes into your cat's mouth than cleaning up what comes out the other end? Here are some low-cost alternative ways to avoid wasting money on your cat's wastes.

- Instead of costly litter liners, insert the empty litter box into a plastic trash bag and then fill with litter. At disposal time, simply remove the bag and litter, tie, and throw away.

- Instead of using an expensive litter box, purchase a recycling bin with a bifold lid that can be kept half open. Your cat will have no trouble getting into it, and the 16-inch (40-cm) sides will prevent litter and wastes from being kicked or squirted out.

- Another litter box option is an under-the-bed storage box of heavy plastic. The sides are about 10 inches (25 cm) high and the lid can be placed under the box for extra floor protection. They cost about 5 dollars.

- If your cat overshoots her box, place her litter box inside a high-sided, cardboard box that you've lined with shelf paper. This idea is also useful if you must place the box in a more visible area of your home.

- Instead of litter, use garage floor oil absorbent, which is cheaper than cat box filler. Oil absorbent is available at hardware and automotive stores.

Scratch Posts

Providing your cat with something of her own to scratch is far less costly than buying new furniture because Kitty sank her claws into your sofa or chairs once too often. Instead of buying an expensive scratching post for your cat, try making your own for less money.

• Cover a 1 inch × 4 inch × 15 inch (2.5 cm × 10 cm × 38 cm) board with a swatch of indoor or indoor/outdoor carpet or wrap it with sisal rope. Use a staple gun, tacks, or nails to fasten the carpet to the board at each end. Attach a piece of rope to the top, and hang the scratch post over a door.

• Wrap sisal rope around a basement support pole, and fasten it with a hot glue gun or tie it at both ends for a quick climbing pole for your cat.

• Wrap a wooden electric-cable spool with carpet. Sit it in front of the television so your cat can watch her favorite kitty video.

• Some cats enjoy clawing wood. Split a log in half so that the bottom is flat. Set the log, flat side down, onto a piece of carpet or newspaper for a quick scratching apparatus.

• For a great multilevel cat tree, buy a wooden ladder, some rolls of sisal rope, and some carpet squares. Cut the carpet to size with a utility knife. Cover the ladder's steps, tacking them on the undersides with a staple gun or carpet tacks. Wrap the sisal around the vertical supports of the ladder, and staple or tack the ends to the wood.

Building this cat climbing apparatus will cost under $100, which is about half of what you might have to pay for a manufactured, multilevel cat tree.

• Cut corrugated cardboard strips the length and height of a shoe box. Fill the shoe box tightly with the cardboard strips. Sprinkle a little catnip onto it, and place it onto the floor.

• Attach carpet with screws or a staple gun to an inconspicuous wall of your house on which your cat can scratch.

Cost-Saving Resources

For information about cost-saving tips, check out this title:

Maggitti, Phil, "Before You Buy That Kitten," Barron's Educational Series, Inc., 1995.

SPAY/USA
1-800-248-SPAY
www.spayusa.org

You will receive information about the nearest low-cost program and will be sent a certificate as proof you have gone through the SPAY/USA network.

Safety Tips

If your cat has a close call with an automobile, she will have no air bag handy to protect her. If your mild-mannered cat comes into contact with a wild-mannered animal, she may become a victim rather than victorious. Even if your cat has been vaccinated, contracting a disease for which there is no defense may be a bitter pill to swallow. Indoor living greatly reduces the threat to our cats that living in the outdoors carries with it. Traffic, contagious diseases, inhumane and abusive people, wild animals, and starvation are just some of the dangers a free-roaming cat must face on a daily basis. While our homes are not entirely free of potential hazards, keeping cats confined inside or allowing them outside only under our control and supervision increases their safety. The life span of an indoor cat is nearly double that of one that lives outdoors or is allowed to roam at her owner's discretion. We can further eliminate potential hazards by making our homes safer places in which our cats can live.

Hazards Around the House

One of the best ways to ensure your indoor cat's safety is to pet proof your home. Like child proofing, pet proofing is making a clean sweep of every room that your cat has access to and removing or concealing anything that presents a potential danger. Some items may be dangerous to one pet while not to another. For example, electric cords may be dangerous to the cat that enjoys chewing. However, for a cat that is not into sharpening her teeth on household objects, electric cords may pose no threat. You may detect other potential hazards once you have discovered what activities turn your cat on.

• Keep small items, such as rubber bands, coins, paper clips, staples, nails, screws, pieces of string, yarn, thread, or dental floss, earrings and other small jewelry, bells, small balls, sewing needles, pins, and the eyes cats may pull off toys, out of your cat's reach.

• When windows are open during the warm months to let in the summer breezes, keep interior doors blocked with a heavy doorstop to prevent them from slamming shut on your pet.

• Some cats hog the heat and lie on floor heating grates to warm their bones. To prevent your cat from being trapped, purchase an elastic or breakaway collar to wear indoors so she can pull away if her tags becomes caught in the grate.

• To keep your cat from chewing electric wires, buy plastic decorator shower rod covers and insert the wires inside the rod covers. Rod covers can be cut to size.

• Alternatively, purchase plastic strips designed to conceal wires that run across floors, across baseboards, and up walls. Concealment strips are available in hardware or office supply stores. They come in a variety of colors and can be cut to size.

• A power strip with a brain protects cats from being electrocuted if they puncture an electric cord with their teeth or claws. The strip detects insulation aging, damage, and penetration and will shut off to prevent serious shock. Check your local hardware or builder's supply store.

• Sew a large pompom to your toilet seat cover to prevent the lid from staying up in case you forget to lower it. This will keep your cat from drinking the water.

• Although a Mr. Yuk sticker won't mean anything to Fluffy, having them on dangerous household chemicals might remind you to put the chemicals away when finished.

• Keep human medicines in closed containers out of your cat's reach, and never give your cat human medicine unless advised to do so by your veterinarian.

• Never give your cat alcoholic beverages. Alcohol can poison your cat.

• If your cat gets any fiberglass insulation on her coat, she may ingest it when washing herself. To protect your cat, keep the insulation contained.

• Put both ironing boards and irons away as soon as you are finished ironing.

• Keep all screen doors fastened and screens secure in their sockets.

• Keep insecticides out of your cat's reach.

• If your cat is small enough, she can become caught in miniblind cords and accidentally strangle. To prevent a tragic accident, mount a cord cleat device next to your miniblind and wrap the excess cord around it.

• To keep your cat from accidentally suffocating to death in the clothes dryer, keep the door closed.

• The opening created by extending the footrest on a recliner chair is another favorite sleeping spot. A cat that has crept inside risks being trapped or crushed when the chair is returned to an upright position. Other places that may unexpectedly harm your cat are inside the lining of an upholstered chair or sofa or in a foldaway bed. Always be extremely cautious when closing any of these.

• If you live in a high-rise apartment, keep windows and screens secure. Falling from upper-story windows occurs so commonly that it has been given a name—*high-rise syndrome*. Do not let your cat become a victim of this kind of tragedy.

• After you have removed that roast beef or tuna casserole from the oven, make certain you have closed the oven door. Cats can burn their feet if they jump onto a hot oven door that is left open.

• If you allow your cat to play in a shopping bag, cut the handles in the middle to prevent them from trapping your cat.

Cats and Antifreeze

Antifreeze will keep your car's engine running in winter, but it may shut down your cat's motor. Because of its sweet taste, antifreeze is appealing both to dogs and cats. If ingested, though, antifreeze is lethal. Traditionally, antifreeze has been made with ethylene glycol, a highly toxic substance that converts to oxalic acid after ingestion. Oxalic acid damages the kidneys and can cause kidney failure and death. Because of its harmful potential, manufacturers have introduced antifreeze made of propylene glycol instead of ethylene glycol. Often, however, these products are referred to as safe or nontoxic in spite of the wording on the products' labels. The unfortunate truth is, however, that *no antifreeze*, regardless of its formula, is completely safe. Antifreeze made from propylene glycol is safer in that it requires ingesting greater amounts before toxicity occurs, but poisoning and death can result if enough of it is ingested. When dealing with antifreeze, caution is the best strategy. Cleaning up spills and preventing your cat from coming into contact with antifreeze is the best way to protect your cat from harm no matter which kind of antifreeze you use.

Escaping the Safety of Your Home

Does your cat want to run outside with your children every time they open the door? Are you afraid that your cat will accidentally take flight whenever someone leaves or enters your house? If locking the door is not an option to keep your cat from bolting through it, try some of these suggestions to keep your cat indoors where she belongs.

• If you do not have double doors or a screen/storm door in addition to a wooden or metal door, install a baby gate on the exterior of the door to prevent your cat from escaping when you leave or enter your home.

• Keep a squirt gun handy by the door. Lightly spray your cat if she appears to be contemplating a break.

• Try clicker-style obedience training, which works for cats as well as for dogs. If your pet knows what *stay* or *sit* mean when you open a door, your pet is less likely to leave with you.

HOW-TO: Find a Lost Cat

Before you begin combing the neighborhood looking for your cat, make sure your cat is not trapped or hiding somewhere in your home. Cats are notorious for finding the most out-of-the-way place to hide. Bring along a smelly treat to get a hiding cat's attention. Once you have determined that your cat is missing, don't wait until your cat decides to come home. The awful truth is that most do not. Among the cats that are turned over to shelters, most are never claimed. Follow these steps to find a lost cat.

1. *Make copies of your cat's photo, include her name and your phone number.*
2. *Talk to everybody in the neighborhood, and leave a copy of the mini-poster with them.*
3. *To entice your cat to come home, place articles of clothing with your scent on them outside your house. Place some of her bedding and some special foods with the clothing.*
4. *Call local veterinarians and emergency clinics in case your cat was injured and taken for treatment.*
5. *Shelters are often required by law to hold pets for a certain number of days for owners to claim them. Make daily shelter visits to view the animals yourself instead of calling on the telephone because shelter staff may not be aware of new animals and what they look like.*
6. *Post flyers of your cat in businesses and shops within a 1-mile (1.6-km) radius of your home or where your cat was lost.*
7. *Place an ad in your local newspaper, and check the pet lost-and-found sections daily.*
8. *Call the National Lost Pet Hotline, 900-535-1515, or the National Found Pet Hotline, 800-755-8111.*
9. *Contact the on-line Missing Pets Network, a virtual linking of Web sites provided by the U.S. Department of Agriculture, where you may post a lost pet notice. In most cases, your post will appear on the Web site within 24 hours. Visit the page at web3.aphis.usda.gov/mpn/anlost.html or access it via the USDA Animal Care Network at www.aphis.usda.gov/reac/achome.html.*

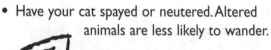

• Have your cat spayed or neutered. Altered animals are less likely to wander.

• Having a collar and identification tags is the quickest way for someone who has found your pet to locate you. When a cat is lost, however, she may lose her collar or tags, so having a secondary form of ID is advisable. Discuss with your veterinarian the options of having your cat tattooed or a microchip implanted. A tattoo involves imprinting on your cat a series of numbers and/or letters. The tattoo ID is then entered into a database, and the cat owner is given a tag for the cat's collar that has the toll-free number to help identify the cat and you as the cat's owner. If the tag is lost, anyone finding your cat can contact a shelter or veterinarian to help identify the animal. Microchips are implanted by a veterinarian under the cat's skin. Like the tattoo, the chip's code is entered into a national database. Special scanners identify a lost cat with an implanted microchip.

In Case of Emergency

Emergency preparedness is one of those things we deal with to manage the situations we never think we will encounter. Even in the most cat-friendly home or with the most conscientious and caring owner, cats can experience accidents. A knowledge of first aid techniques and a well-stocked emergency kit may make the difference between life and death for your cat. Just about any cat could have any type of accident, but some occur more frequently than others depending on the species. Common feline emergencies include burns, cuts, animal bites, puncture wounds, electric shock, ingesting poisons and poisonous plants, ingesting rodenticides and insecticides, injuries due to falling, choking, and, if your cat goes outside, frostbite and heatstroke. Prepare yourself for an emergency by following these guidelines.

• Keep your veterinarian's phone number near your telephone.

• Know how your veterinarian handles emergency situations after regular business hours. If your veterinarian has no emergency service after hours, know the name, telephone number, and location of the nearest veterinary emergency clinic. Keep copies of your cat's medical records, especially if it has a health condition, in the event you must use an emergency clinic.

• Purchase a book about pet first aid, and be familiar with basic first aid techniques.

• Have available a first aid kit. If you prefer, purchase a prepackaged first aid kit designed for pets. Available at pet stores are first aid kits that enable you to keep all necessary first aid items handy in one package. Although more expensive than making your own, prepackaged kits are more convenient.

• Find out if your local Red Cross chapter offers training in first aid for pets, and take their course if one is available.

• In the event of poisoning, know the telephone number and procedures of the ASPCA National Animal Poison Control Center (NAPCC). This is a division of the American Society for the Prevention of Cruelty to Animals (ASPCA) and is the first animal-oriented poison control center in the United States. The center is an allied agency of the University of Illinois College of Veterinary Medicine. You may visit the ASPCA/NAPCC web site for information about the organization at *www.napcc.aspca.org/. Do not visit the web site when you have a poison-related emergency. You need to call your veterinarian or the National Animal Poison Control Center directly.*

Incredible, Inedible Greens

Your houseplants may be a source of visual pleasure for you. However, for the cat that enjoys sinking her teeth into them, houseplants may be a source of danger. Many common houseplants are toxic to pets. Symptoms of ingestion range from nausea, diarrhea, and vomiting to convulsions and death. Not bringing poisonous plants into the home is the best way to protect your cat. However, if you have any poisonous plants, keep them out of your cat's reach.

• To obtain a complete list of poisonous plants, write to the American Society of Prevention of Cruelty to Animals/National Animal Poison Control Center (ASPCA/NAPCC), 1717 South Philo Road, Suite #36, Urbana, IL 61802. Enclose a check for $20 dollars payable to NAPCC. The 67-page bound publication is indexed and includes sections about toxic, potentially toxic, and nontoxic plants. It summarizes information from research sources and the ASPCA/NAPCC case database.

HOW-TO: Make Your Own First Aid Kit

Learn the proper first aid techniques. Keep your first aid kit well stocked, and replenish items when they dwindle or expire. Label the kit. Keep it in a dry, accessible location. Include the following.

Tweezers, both blunt tipped and pointed, for the removal of ticks or objects stuck in your cat's paws or skin.

A magnifying glass to help you see small objects imbedded in wounds or in your cat's skin.

Cotton balls and cotton swabs to clean wounds.

3% hydrogen peroxide for cleaning wounds with pus or scabs.

Antibiotic ointment to apply to wounds following cleaning with hydrogen peroxide.

Nonstick bandages and pads for covering cuts, abrasions, and wounds.

Gauze bandages (1 inch (2.5 cm) and 3 inch (8 cm)) to wrap wounds or muzzle a panicky cat that might bite you if she is excited or in pain. Don't muzzle a cat that is having difficulty breathing. As an alternative, keep a cat muzzle in your first aid kit.

Adhesive tape (1 inch (2.5 cm)) to secure a bandage.

Scissors to clip the hair around a wound and to cut adhesive tape and bandages.

• Another great source for poisonous plant information is the Cornell University Poisonous Plants web page at *www.ansci.cornell.edu/plants/plants.html/*. The Cornell page includes summaries of the literature and references for each plant, pictures of the plants, the types of poisons present, diagnosis and prevention of animal poisoning, species affected by each plant, and pictures of affected animals. The page also has links to other web pages of toxic plants.

• As an alternative, ask your veterinarian for a list of poisonous plants or check out a book from your local library.

Disaster Preparedness

At various times of the year, depending on where we live, Mother Nature casts her wrath and fury upon us in the form of tornadoes, hurricanes, floods, fires, earthquakes, snowstorms, and even volcanoes. Add to the mix man-made emergencies such as

Cardboard to make an Elizabethan-style collar to keep your cat from licking the wounds or pulling off the bandages.

Clean towels and cloths to stop bleeding.

Styptic pencil to stop bleeding.

Pet carrier to help carry the animal to your local veterinarian.

Milk of magnesia or *charcoal tablets* for poisonings. **Caution: Do not treat your pet for poison unless you are advised to do so by a veterinarian or by the ASPCA/National Animal Poison Control Center.**

The ASPCA/NAPCC recommends the addition of the following items to your pet first aid kit so that you can handle an emergency that involves poisons or contamination by a toxic substance.

Turkey baster, bulb syringe, or large medicine syringe to apply solutions.

Saline eye solution to flush out eye contaminants.

Mild *grease-cutting dishwashing liquid* to bathe an animal after skin contamination.

Rubber gloves to prevent you from being exposed to the poisonous agent while you bathe your cat to remove the contaminating substance.

chemical spills, explosions, or nuclear power disasters, and the potential for wreaking havoc on our lives escalates. In most cases, disaster centers do not allow pets to wait out the problem with their owners. Often, the family pet is forgotten under such circumstances and left behind to fend for herself until her human family returns. Unfortunately, many pets do not survive the disaster, or they become stranded only to be rescued by strangers and never reunited with those they love. Some disasters, such as floods, may last for several weeks. Others, such as snowstorms, may simply keep us from getting to the grocery store for a few days. Whatever the potential for disaster in your geographic locale, knowing what to do with your cat will help her survive.

• Always take your cat with you, or board her at a safe location outside the disaster area. Never leave your cat alone in the home with food and water. Animals can become disoriented and panicked in times of crises. They can upset their water or food bowls. If a door collapses or a window blows in, your cat can easily escape. If a wall or roof caves in, your cat could be crushed and die. In a flood, your cat could drown.

• If you travel frequently and might be away when disaster strikes, having a buddy in the neighborhood who will look after your cat may be her only chance of survival.

• Put a collar and identification tag on your cat that includes your name and phone number in case your cat becomes lost or stranded.

• Keep your cat's vaccinations current.

• Know the locations of animal shelters in your area in case you have to visit them if your cat becomes lost. If your pet is lost, call the National Lost Pet Hotline, 900-535-1515, or the National Found Pet Hotline, 800-755-8111.

• Contact friends or relatives outside the disaster area for temporary placement of your cat.

• Prepare a list of veterinarians and boarding facilities that might be able to board your cat.

• Contact pet-friendly hotels and motels outside the disaster area that might be able to house you and your cat.

• Keep the results of your research handy, such as relevant phone numbers and contacts.

• Keep a disaster kit on hand or purchase one. Check your pet stores or mail order catalogs for ready-made kits, or make your own as described below.

Moving Day

Moving to a new home or apartment can be an exciting adventure or an unwanted upheaval. Cats typically do not cope well with change. Older cats are even more rigid and may have a more difficult time adjusting to moving than younger cats. So, make the change as stress free for your cat as possible by following these simple hints.

HOW-TO: Make a Disaster Kit for Your Cat

1. Include at least one month's supply of cat food, a can opener (if necessary), food and water bowls, airtight containers for dry food, some of your cat's favorite treats, a supply of paper towels, antibacterial hand wipes, and several gallons (liters) of bottled water. Store the items in covered plastic trash cans that will fit inside your car or its trunk. If you have a storm cellar or shelter in your home, store the cat necessities along with your own.
2. Pack a month's supply of litter, a litter box and scoop, and a supply of waste disposal bags.
3. Pack some familiar bedding, toys, and grooming tools. Your cat will be just as stressed as you.
4. Have on hand a backup supply of your cat's medication, such as insulin, as well as the necessary tools to administer the medication, such as needles, syringes, or pill guns.
5. Include your first aid kit.
6. Include your cat's medical records and a current photo.
7. Include a carrier or crate for each cat and a strong harness and leash.

- If you are moving to a new apartment or condominium, make certain pets are allowed before taking the leap. If no pets rules are in effect, consider moving elsewhere rather than giving up your feline companion. Having to adjust to a new owner, assuming one can be found, will be more traumatic for your cat than adjusting to a new home with you in it.

- If you are having your belongings professionally moved, keep your cat out of the way. Movers carrying heavy boxes or pieces of furniture will be more concerned about tripping over a cat than they will be about stepping on her. For your cat's safety and that of the movers, confine her on packing and moving day.

HOW-TO: Make Certain Someone Else Knows About Your Cat

If someone besides you had to provide care for your cat if an emergency occurred that kept you from doing so, would he or she be able to? Would the person know what your cat eats, when she eats, and any odd eating habits she has? Would the person know what kind of litter your cat prefers? Would the temporary caregiver know if she has any health problems or even who her veterinarian is? One of the ways you can help a relative, friend, or neighbor give your cat temporary care when you can't is to make a folder that tracks your cat's history. The folder should contain descriptions of your cat, up-to-date health and behavior data, and any other useful information that will ensure that she continues to get proper care if you are incapacitated. A cat folder is also useful to take along if you are traveling with your cat and must obtain emergency veterinary care on the trip.

1. *Designate a specific individual as your cat's emergency caregiver. Keep the person's name and phone number in your wallet as well as instructions to notify that person if something happens to you.*
2. *Buy a pocket folder at an office supply store, and instruct your cat's temporary caregiver where it will be kept. Show your cat's caregiver where you keep your cat's food and other necessities.*
3. *Place a photo of your cat inside the folder.*

• If you are packing your own belongings, make sure your cat doesn't get packed inside a box with your clothing or other items. Cats will be inclined to explore any boxes you have in the home prior to moving and curl up in them to take a nap.

• Take your cat to your new home before you move into it so she can become familiar with the place. Your cat will appreciate being part of the process and be more comfortable in her new home if she has been given the chance to explore it before making a permanent leap.

4. List important information such as her birth date, breed, sex, color, and markings.
5. Include your veterinarian's name, address, and phone number.
6. Summarize important medical information, and keep it current. Place your veterinarian receipts, health certificates, and the summary into the folder.
7. Indicate any medications the cat is taking and how often.
8. If your cat is battling a long-term illness, track her symptoms on a daily basis and keep the list in the folder.
9. Make a list of important feeding information. Include the number and times of daily feedings; types, brands, and quantities of food; and any food allergies or problem reactions, such as certain types or brands causing diarrhea.
10. Make a list of any noteworthy personality information, such as the cat not liking men or women or children. Describe if the cat has any problems with other animals or species. List whether the cat has any idiosyncratic bathroom habits, such as urinating over the side of the litter box.
11. Make certain your cat's backup caregiver knows where the folder containing all this information is kept in the event of an emergency.

Holiday Safety

Like moving to a new home, surviving the holidays may take some special consideration for your cat. Lots of visitors who might leave the door open a little too long when they enter or leave, new and unusual gastronomic delights that tempt a cat looking for a quick change in her diet, the presence of decorations that, to most cats, look like great playthings, or discarded boxes and crumpled wrapping paper that might conceal a kitten are just a few of the hazards prevalent at holidays. To make the end-of-the-year holidays a wonderful time for both the two- and four-legged members of your family, follow these suggestions.

HOW-TO: Have a Cat-Safe Holiday Tree

Creating a holiday tree that is both beautiful to look at for you and unattractive to your cat is a special challenge. The following are a baker's dozen suggestions to keep your tree cat-friendly.

1. *Keep your cat from drinking the tree water by covering the tree basin with foil or a tree skirt.*
2. *Place cat-safe ornaments made from cloth, wood, fiber, or wicker near the bottom of the tree in case Fluffy decides to use the ornaments as playthings.*
3. *Tie up the lights' loose electric cords, and keep them concealed by attaching them with wire or cord to the trunk of the tree. End-to-end lights eliminate individual cords dangling from the tree that might entice your cat to chew on them.*
4. *If you have lots of tree lights that are not end to end, purchase a power strip on which to plug the lights. Attach the strip to the tree trunk at a level that is higher than the height of your cat. As a result, you will have only one heavy-duty power cord running from the tree to the outlet instead of several flimsy cords from single strings of lights.*
5. *Decorate with steady-burning lights rather than bubble-style lights because the motion of the bubbles inside the glass tubes and blinking lights are fascinating to cats.*
6. *To prevent your cat from knocking over your holiday tree, anchor it with cord or wire to the ceiling directly above the tree's trunk. Do not attach it with wire to a wall behind the tree because your cat could get caught in the wire if she runs behind the tree.*
7. *An artificial tree will help discourage the climbing cat because it has nothing for your cat to sink her claws into and climb to the top. If you opt for a live tree, get one with thick foliage to discourage the climber.*
8. *Spray the lower branches of the tree with bitter apple, cinnamon, lemon, eucalyptus, or another unappealing scent to dampen your cat's curiosity.*

• Cover candles with glass chimneys to keep Fluffy from flicking her tail into the flame. Place the covered candles out of the way to keep her from knocking them over and starting a fire.

• Keep a screen in front of your fireplace to keep your cat out of it or from being burned by flying sparks.

• Plants, such as English holly, Jerusalem cherry, amaryllis, and mistletoe, are poisonous to pets. Keep them out of your cat's reach, or, better yet,

9. Hang your ornaments with ribbons rather than hooks to keep your cat from accidentally swallowing something that could get lodged in her throat.

10. Angel hair, made of glass fiber, and tinsel, made of metal, can cause internal damage if your cat swallows any. Do not place these near the bottom of the tree.

11. Avoid decorating your tree with strings of berries or other edible ornaments. Many are harmful to cats if swallowed. The string on which they are attached can cause damage to your cat's intestines if swallowed.

12. If you like, decorate a small, artificial tree for your cat with items your cat will find appealing. Cats will love having a tree full of catnip toys, stuffed toys, and containers of kitty treats. Hide the tree until you are ready for your cat to open her presents.

13. If nothing you do will keep your cat away from your tree, try some of the following cat-safe alternatives to trimming a tree.

   a. Decorate a mantel or dining room buffet with miniature evergreens or artificial tree boughs trimmed with fruit, nuts, or dried seed pods.

   b. Hang garland above door frames or around picture frames and mirrors.

   c. Decorate a two-dimensional tree made from grape vines, rattan, or fake greenery. They are designed to hang from the wall and are available at craft stores.

   d. Decorate an outdoor tree. Place food items onto it for the birds and squirrels. Your cat will have loads of fun watching the wildlife.

   e. Decorate a tree in a room that is off-limits to your cat.

don't bring them home. Poinsettias, which have had a bad reputation, are no longer considered toxic.

• Keep your cat away from poultry bones that can splinter and lodge in her digestive system.

• Make certain guests are aware of your cat and don't accidentally let her out.

• Do not let your cat imbibe in holiday cheer. As little as 1 ounce (30 ml) of alcohol can cause poisoning. Drunken pets are not any funnier than drunken people, and they may end up dead.

Safety Resources

The ASPCA/National Animal Poison Control Center (*www.napcc.aspca.org*)

Because the ASPCA/NAPCC is a non-profit organization, a fee is charged in order to offset a portion of the cost of providing the vital service. If you have a poisoning emergency, dial 1-800-548-2423 or 1-888-4ANIHELP (1-888-426-4435). The cost for assistance is $45 dollars per case with no extra charge for follow-up calls. You must use Visa, MasterCard, Discover, or American Express when you call. With 800/888 access only, the ASPCA/NAPCC will do as many follow-up calls as necessary in critical cases, and, at the owner's request, will consult his or her veterinarian. Alternatively, dial 1-900-680-0000, and the $45 dollar fee per case will appear on your telephone bill.

When you call the ASPCA/NAPCC, be ready to provide your name, address, and telephone number; any information concerning the exposure to the poison, including the type and brand of the poisonous substance; the quantity ingested or contacted, if known; the time since the exposure; the breed, age, sex, weight, and number of animals involved; and the symptoms your pet is experiencing.

Keep one of these first aid books or videos handy. Familiarize yourself with treating common emergencies.

Mammato, Bobbie, DVM, MPH, "Pet First Aid: Cats and Dogs," The American Red Cross and The Humane Society of the United States, Hanover, MD: Mosby Consumer Health and Safety, 1997.

"Pet First Aid," Apogee Entertainment, 159 Alpine Way, 1-888-360-9966.

Schwartz, Stefanie, "First Aid for Cats: An Owner's Guide to a Happy, Healthy Pet," IDG Books, 1998.

For the story about a woman who rescues animals in times of disaster, read:

Crisp, Terri, and Samantha Glen, "Out of Harm's Way," Pocket Books, 1996.

For stories about animals lost or turned over to shelters, read:

Hess, Elizabeth, "Lost and Found: Dogs, Cats, and Everyday Heroes at a Country Animal Shelter," Harcourt Brace and Company, 1998.

Feeding Tips

When the hungries hit, we can choose to pull something out of the refrigerator or head to the nearest restaurant for our meals. Our cats don't have those options. Food that has become stale and moldy or overcome with ants or other bugs, water that has been sitting too long or in the wrong location, and even zits from oily food bowls are some of the food-related problems our cats may have to face every day. If your cat is trying to tell you something about her eating and drinking options, here are some suggestions for improving her vital victuals.

Armies of Ants

No matter how clean your kitchen is, ants may find it attractive. No matter how careful you are about not dropping bits of food onto the floor or not losing them between appliances and furniture cushions, you may find armies of ants marching into your home like they are at a holiday picnic. If you are troubled by ants devouring your cat's food before she does, here are several ways to discourage ants from overrunning her dinner.

• Place your cat's bowls of food inside slightly larger bowls or saucers filled with water. Ants do not swim and will not cross the water to get to the food. In fact, you may find that they will send out the word to their ant friends and stop coming into your house altogether.

• Purchase one of the new, molded-plastic ant-proof bowls that has a saucer to hold water and keep ants at bay. Check your local pet store, on-line pet site, or one of the mail order catalogs listed in the last chapter of this book.

• Putting your cat's dry food into containers will not only help keep it fresh but will also help keep your neighborhood's ant population from carrying it off to feed their families.

• Do not leave your cat's uneaten wet food sitting around to attract other bugs. Feed only portions she can eat within 20-30 minutes, then clean the dish.

• Tansy is a natural ant repellent. Set containers of dried tansy around your kitchen to keep the ants out. By using tansy as an ant repellent, you will not have to worry about dangerous chemical bug repellents that can be harmful to your cat if she ingests them. Check your local health food or herb store, or grow tansy and dry it at the end of the growing season. *A word of caution, however. Tansy takes over a garden, so grow it in a pot in a sunny location. Tansy regenerates year after year.*

• To keep armies of ants from devouring your cat's (or your) food, find the ants' entry point and sprinkle dried mint or red pepper at the spot.

The Food's Out of the Bag

Does your cat like dry food when you first open a new bag of it, then turn her nose up at it when the bag is about half empty? Has your cat's dry food become stale or moisture laden from sitting around too long in your cupboard, basement, or garage? The tasty morsels that made Muffy's mouth water when you first bought them can lose their flavor and savor because they have become stale and moldy. This is especially true if your home is damp or if you keep your windows open during warm weather. These helpful hints will help keep your cat's taste buds satisfied and your wallet from emptying faster than her container of dry food.

• To keep dry food fresh after opening the container, pour the contents of the bag or box into a plastic or tin airtight container. Store it in a cool, dry place.

• The food that was grown and made into your cat's food had all of the sunlight it needed when it was in the fields. Now that it's been processed, keeping it away from direct sunlight will help keep it fresh and prevent the oils that are in it from heating up and becoming rancid.

• If you have just bought a big supply of your cat's favorite dry food so you could use up those store coupons before they expired, place some of the food into a container and put it in your freezer. Alternatively, place the entire bag or box of dry cat food in your freezer if it will fit. When the time arrives to feed it to Peaches, get it out of the freezer a few hours ahead of time so it will thaw. Place the unused portion into a sealed container to keep it fresh.

• Some products on the market will help you keep those large bags sealed tight as the bag empties. Scoop N Seal is available at pet stores.

• Close bags of dry cat food with a bag clip. Bag clips come in different sizes for different-sized bags. If you have a home office, perhaps you have some binder clips that will work just as well.

• If you open a bag or box of dry cat food and find it laden with little bugs, chances are that the food expired because it sat in your home or on a grocer's shelf too long. The bug larvae were in the ingredients of your cat's food when it came from the fields. By being so tiny that they escaped the food-processing equipment, the larvae eventually hatched. You will find the expiration date on containers of dry food, so check the dates before purchasing.

Gobbling the Greens

No one knows exactly why cats do it, but they frequently can be seen chomping on grass. Some motivation may be the result of instinctive behavior because greens are a normal part of a wild carnivore's diet when she feeds on a herbivore with a full stomach. Often, a cat swallows the grass whole, and a small episode of vomiting follows. Eating grass may provide some type of nourishment, or the chlorophyll in the grass may settle a cat's stomach. So providing some greens for your cat may aid her digestive process.

• Clip off some green grass that is chemical-free and bring it into the house for your cat to eat. Rinse the grass before offering it to your cat.

• Keep a container of lettuce in the refrigerator. Cover the lettuce with water. Pour some of the water into a bowl daily for your cat to drink.

• Pour the liquid off of steamed or boiled green vegetables. Pour the cooled liquid over some dry kibble or into a water dish for your cat to drink.

• If you open a can of vegetables, drain the liquid into your cat's water dish.

• Grow some grass in a small container for your cat to nibble on when the spirit moves her.

• Purchase some prepackaged grass intended just for Kitty.

More Than a Meal

With some cats, meals are not the only source of oral intake. Wool and other fibers, nondigestible plant material, rubber, plastic, wood, and even her own hair are just some of the things a cat may choose to ingest. Pica—the drive to consume material that is not generally considered food—is what animal behaviorists call a compulsive disorder. Compulsive disorders are competitive, nonfunctional, nonbeneficial behaviors. In a human, examples of compulsive disorders include repetitive and frequent hand washing or pulling one's hair out. Although the exact cause of compulsive disorders is unknown, animal behaviorists feel that they are often caused by stress brought on by environmental conflicts such as competition with other pets, changes in the home, constant punishment, or confinement to small areas such as cages or crates. Lack of socialization or too much attention may bring about a compulsive behavior. A nutritionally imbalanced diet may also lead to pica. A cat with a compulsive disorder loses control over her ability to initiate and stop these negative, repetitive actions. Often the compulsive behaviors are oral in nature, causing the cat to eat things she should not.

• The first step in treating a compulsive disorder is to identify the cause and eliminate it. For example, if your cat is caged or crated for a large portion of the day, allowing her outside the confined space will help get the cat on the road to recovery.

• Do not reinforce your cat by paying attention to her while she is engaged in the compulsive behavior. Providing good, quality time on a set schedule is preferable and more effective than petting, stroking, or verbally consoling your cat in the midst of repetitive activity.

• Do not punish your cat for the compulsive behavior or for other inappropriate activities. This will not prevent a compulsive behavior from developing or it may make the cat fearful of you.

• Provide something for your cat to chew on. Even cats will respond to being offered a pig ear or piece of rawhide.

• Spray household objects your cat likes to chew on with cayenne pepper; essential oils in citrus, cinnamon, or eucalyptus scents; spray deodorant; or perfume that is not a scent you use.

• Spray favorite chewables with a pet repellent to deter your cat from sticking nonfood objects into her mouth.

- Keep dangerous objects such as yarn or string out of your cat's reach to prevent her from chewing and swallowing them.

- If your cat is chewing her hair, she may have an allergy. Discuss the problem with your veterinarian before embarking on a behavior modification program.

- Add fiber to your cat's diet by mixing her food with vegetables or bran.

- As a last resort to solve a compulsive eating disorder, discuss drug therapy with your veterinarian. Drugs that increase serotonin levels and some antidepressants are used for treating compulsive disorders including compulsive eating.

- Wool chewing is one of the most common types of pica in cats and is most often found among the Siamese or Burmese varieties. Keep your woolens out of your cat's reach.

- Provide your wool-sucking cat with her own chew toys.

Kitty Zits

Zits. Yes, believe it or not, cats can develop them just as a person can. Feline acne can develop on your cat's face, chin, and lower lip. It appears like small black spots that, if not washed regularly, may turn into crusty patches that cake and bleed. Your cat will not worry about her acne preventing her from getting a date. However, she may be bothered if the acne builds up and she tries to scratch it off with her toenails, causing the area to bleed and possibly turn raw. While most human acne is limited to the teenagers among the species, feline acne can affect cats of any age. Cats with oily skin are more susceptible to getting acne than their drier-skinned counterparts, and a cat's food bowl may be part of the problem.

- Kitty zits are more annoying than serious. Keep your cat's chin clean and free of the unsightly blemishes by gently washing it with a soft cloth and warm water once or twice a day. If the area has begun to bleed, wash it with some hydrogen peroxide on a cotton ball to fight infection.

• Plastic food bowls retain oils that can add to your cat's acne problem, since her chin rubs against the bowl when she is busy snarfing down dinner. Replace those oil-ridden plastic bowls with aluminum, glass, or lead-free pottery and china bowls.

• Wash your cat's food bowls daily with a mild dish detergent to remove oily deposits.

Water, Water Everywhere . . .

. . . and not a drop to drink. Is evaporation the only reason the water in your cat's water bowl diminishes? Does your cat pester to drink from a sink faucet? For humans, having a drink of water when we eat complements our meal. For cats, drinking and eating go together about as well as stripes and plaids. Yet, water is a fundamental building block of nutrition. Without it, cats, like humans, can become dehydrated and sick. If your cat turns her nose up at drinking from the water bowl, here are some suggestions for encouraging her to drink.

• Use separate food and water bowls for your cat instead of pet dishes that combine the two. Place her water dish away from her food bowl either in the same room or in another room entirely.

• If your cat likes to drink from the faucet, place a water dish near her favorite watering hole.

• Your cat may prefer icy cold water to water that is room temperature. Keep a gallon (liter) container of water in the refrigerator, and refill her dish periodically.

- Place an ice cube or two into her water dish daily.

- If your cat gets a snout full when she tries to drink from a bowl, she could have a vision problem. To help her know where the waterline is, use a ceramic bowl with a pattern on it.

- If your cat likes to drink from the toilet, provide an alternative drinking spot in your bathroom. Toilet cleaners can leave residues that could harm your cat. A small kitten or cat could fall into the toilet and drown.

While the Owner's Away

Does your cat go on a temporary hunger strike when she is boarded or while you are away? Being without the person she is accustomed to or being in a strange environment can cause a cat to feel discomfort and stress that results in a loss of appetite. If you plan to board your cat or hire a pet sitter to care for her in your home, here are some suggestions to pass along to keep your cat's digestive juices flowing.

- If you leave your cat at home with a pet sitter, be sure to alert the sitter to the possibility of her not eating. A good sitter will ask you for relevant medical information when you sign the pet-sitting contract. However, make sure he or she knows the name and phone number of your cat's veterinarian and how to contact you if an eating problem develops.

- Along with your cat's regular food, leave some tempting foods such as chicken or turkey to offer her. Keep your cat's favorite treats on hand.

- Instruct the pet sitter to put measured quantities of food in the bowl so he or she can tell if your cat is eating.

- If your cat still won't eat while you are away, you may have a problem. If not eating occurs for two days, make certain your sitter knows to contact you or your veterinarian.

• If you are boarding your cat at a kennel, there are now products designed to stop spraying behavior in cats, which have also been proven to stimulate a cat's appetite when she is in a new environment. These sprays will help a cat feel more comfortable in boarding situations.

• Provide some cans of people tuna packed in water, the liquid of which can be drained over dry food to make it more appealing.

• Keep on hand some beef, chicken, or turkey baby food (without garlic) or plain yogurt to entice your cat to eat if she goes on a hunger strike.

• If your cat hides from strangers, instruct the sitter to put your cat's food dish where she is hanging out, such as under the bed, to help your cat feel more secure in your absence.

• Call your cat, and leave a message for her on your answering machine.

• Carry a postcard inside your clothing for a few hours, then mail it to your cat. Ask whoever is picking up your mail to let your cat sniff the postcard so she will smell your scent.

Feeding Resources

Check out some of these books about pet food, feeding, and cooking for your cat:

🐱 Davis, Karen Leigh, "Fat Cat, Finicky Cat: A Pet Owner's Guide to Cat Food and Feline Nutrition," Barron's Educational Series, 1997.

🐱 Rees, Wendy Nan, "No Catnapping in the Kitchen: Kitty Cat Cuisine," IDG Books, 1996.

🐱 Thornton, Kim Campbell, and Jane Calloway, "Cat Treats," Doubleday, 1997.

Grooming Tips

Cats as well as cat owners take to the grooming process with varying degrees of acceptance. If your cat balks at a bath or bristles when you wield a brush, the grooming process changes from delight to drudgery. When you adopt a new cat, the time you will have to spend grooming may be a factor in your selection. A Persian or a Birman cat will take more time than an American or a British Shorthair. All cats require some grooming. However, if the time you have to spend is limited, look for a cat with sleeker, shorter hair that is easier to maintain.

Establish a regular grooming routine. Groom your cat at least weekly or more often if conditions (such as fleas, allergies, romping in the mud, and so on) warrant it. Select a place that is convenient for you, and have your grooming tools handy. Make the session a positive experience, and use treats to reward your cat if you like. If you haven't fixed yourself a cup of chamomile tea as preparation for grooming your cat, reward yourself with a cup of it after you finish the job.

Brushing and Combing

Brushing and combing your cat keeps her from developing painful knots that could require the services of a professional groomer to remove. Brushing and combing help you detect the presence of fleas and ticks, and, if combined with a massage, help you detect any lumps or bumps in or under the skin. Brushing and combing your cat also means that if more hair is deposited onto the brush or comb, less hair will be deposited into the environment. When brushing up on your cat's grooming, try some of these helpful hints.

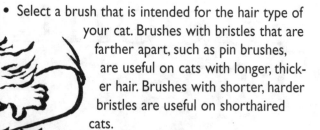

• Select a brush that is intended for the hair type of your cat. Brushes with bristles that are farther apart, such as pin brushes, are useful on cats with longer, thicker hair. Brushes with shorter, harder bristles are useful on shorthaired cats.

• If you have purchased your cat from a breeder, ask the breeder what kind of brush is best to use on the breed.

• Wire brushes and slicker brushes help remove dry, dead skin from your cat's coat along with the excess hair. Getting the hair out of the wire brushes and slickers once you've groomed your cat to a fine luster can be difficult if not impossible. To help remove the hair deposits on the wire brush, use a toothpick between the bristles.

• Try a grooming glove that you wear on your hand. The tiny prongs on the glove's surface remove dead hair as you gently stroke your cat.

• An undercoat rake will help remove the undercoat of hair on your cat that typically knots up. ***Caution: If you are showing your cat, make certain that removing the undercoat of your cat's coat is acceptable for the show ring.***

• Wrap masking tape around your hand, and take the tape lightly over your cat's coat to lift off excess hair.

• Massage your cat with dampened hands to remove excess hair.

• A damp rubber glove will help remove excess hair from your cat as well as your furniture.

• If your cat likes to be massaged, purchase a battery-operated massager or one that also functions as a brush. The gentle sound, similar to a cat's purr, relaxes tension and soothes sore muscles as you groom your cat.

• Vacuuming hair from your cat helps when shedding season arrives and eliminates some of it from attaching to your furniture. Some cats like the vacuum cleaner, while others run from it and hide. To accustom your cat to the vacuum being gently run over her coat, begin using it when your pet is a kitten.

• If burrs have become tangled in your cat's hair, crush them with a pair of pliers before brushing them out. The crushed burrs will not stick to your cat's hair. Another method of removing burrs is first to saturate them with white petroleum jelly or mineral oil, then work them out of your cat's hair with your hands.

• Thinning shears will help you thin your cat's hair during warmer seasons, and they are useful when you must remove knots from your cat's coat. *Caution: If you are showing your cat, make certain that thinning her hair is acceptable for the show ring.*

• If your local pet store doesn't have the right brush or comb for your cat, visit a pet-grooming supply store or a cat show, or order them on-line or through one of the mail-order catalogs listed in the last chapter of this book.

• When brushing and combing your cat, check the skin for signs of dermatitis or parasites. If you detect any problems, see your veterinarian.

• Some of the more skittish kitties may run when they see their owners wielding a brush or comb. If your cat balks at being brushed, use a device that fits into the palm of your hand and is easily concealed from your cat. Since it is made of rubber with tiny rubber projections, the alternative to a hairbrush pulls dead hair from your cat while doing what your cat loves best—petting and stroking.

- Store your cat's grooming tools in a plastic bag with some loose catnip to make the grooming session more appealing.

- Attach a corner grooming brush to a corner where your cat likes to rub her face.

Controlling Fleas and Ticks

Summertime, and the livin' is easy for the tiny insects that feed off your cat. If you see one flea, within a few weeks, you may see hundreds. If you are unlucky, you may also see eggs that hatch before your very eyes in a warm spot, such as where your cat

HOW-TO: Clip Your Cat's Claws

Your cat may resort to biting her nails if you don't trim them regularly. How often to clip your cat's claws will depend on the rate at which they grow. Claw clipping should not be an ordeal, although both you and your cat may think so. The following are some time-tested tips for clipping your cat's nails.

1. Use only nail clippers designed for use on an animal to clip your cat's nails safely. The most popular is the guillotine-style nail clippers. You insert the claw into it, and squeeze the clipper's handles to cut the nail.
2. Use an old laundry bag, a towel, or a pillowcase to restrain your cat if she balks at having her nails clipped. Purchase a device that functions like a mini pet straitjacket and keeps your cat under control when you must clip her nails. The device fits snugly and fastens around your cat with Velcro. Zippered openings allow you to extend one paw at a time for easy nail clipping without the fear of your cat sinking other claws into your skin.
3. Grasp your cat's foot. Press the pads of the foot to extend the claws. If your cat squirms, find someone who can help you hold your cat steady.
4. Slide the clipper onto the nail just below the pink area called the quick. **Caution: Be certain not to cut above the quick (pink area) of your cat's nails. The quick contains nerves and blood. When cut, it is very painful to your pet and will result in bleeding. You will see the quick easily in cats whose nails are light-colored.**
5. Squeeze the clippers to clip off the nail tip with one smooth action.
6. If you accidentally cut through the quick and your cat's nail bleeds, stop the bleeding by holding a clean cloth or cotton swab to the nail. Alternatively, you can apply a little styptic powder or a moistened styptic pencil, or you can dip the nail into some flour to stop the bleeding. If bleeding persists, take your cat to a veterinarian.

sleeps. Ticks, on the other hand, may attach themselves to your cat and go unnoticed until they embed in her skin and potentially cause some real damage. If you live in a warm, humid region of the country, your cat is more inclined to experience flea and tick infestations than if you live in a cooler, drier climate.

Battling these external parasites has become a lot easier in recent years with the development of new flea- and tick-fighting products. However, the best way to ensure that your cat and you don't become overrun by fleas and ticks is never to let your guard down. Check your cat's coat after every romp in the outdoors during flea and tick season, and keep her armed against these pesky critters. Even if your cat stays indoors, she may get fleas from those you carry inside on your clothing. You will commonly notice fleas around your cat's neck, behind her ears, and at the base of her tail. Flecks of flea feces and eggs, which look like salt and pepper, fall off an infested cat and are deposited wherever your cat sits or sleeps. Ticks can land anywhere on your cat, so be sure to brush out your cat's coat after she comes indoors.

If you do get a flea infestation, you must eliminate them from your cat and your home. Adult fleas as well as the eggs and larvae must be destroyed. ***When you select a flea- or tick-fighting product, be certain what species it is intended for. Never use a dog product on a cat, and never combine products.***

• "The best offense is a good defense" goes the old football adage, but it is also true for flea-fighting products. Ask your veterinarian for information about flea busters in pill or liquid form, or any newer topicals for the most effective way to prevent fleas from attacking your cat. Since they were developed to kill flea eggs and larvae as well as adult fleas, these products prevent flea infestations before they start.

• If you are using a flea shampoo to rid your cat of fleas, lather a ring of suds around her neck to keep fleas from running up to her head.

• Flea combs trap fleas in the metal teeth for removal and disposal.

- Another way to pick fleas off of your cat is first to dab your finger in petroleum jelly before manually removing the fleas.

- To get fleas out of your carpet and keep the larvae from hatching, sprinkle the carpet with table salt or borax. Allow this to stand for several hours, then vacuum.

- When vacuuming during a flea infestation, throw away the vacuum cleaner bag after each use to prevent any eggs or larvae you have picked up from hatching and reinfesting your home.

- If you use a fogger or inverted aerosol spray to remove fleas from your home, make sure it has an insect growth regulator (IGR) to kill fleas in all of their life stages.

- To remove ticks, use a blunt-tipped pair of tweezers. Put the tick into a plastic bag. Take it to your veterinarian to analyze what type of tick it is and to discuss the potential of Lyme disease.

Cleaning the Cat

You may have noticed how fastidious your cat companion is. Cats are known for their cleanliness. However, an occasional bath may be necessary if your cat gets into something she shouldn't or if you are planning to exhibit her at a cat show. The hints below will help you get the water onto your cat and your cat into the water.

- Sometimes, getting a job done is as simple as having the right tools, and bathing your cat is no exception. An indoor pet spray that attaches to your sink faucet or showerhead makes bathing your cat easier to manage and provides a gentle spray.

- When rinsing the soap from your cat's coat, use one part vinegar and four parts water. This mixture will leave her coat shiny and clean.

- If your cat just doesn't like the water, use a water-free bath shampoo that must be applied and then lathered into your cat's coat until a foam appears. Brush, and towel dry with a blow-dryer.

• If your cat picked up urine odors from rubbing against the interior sides of a covered litter box, rub some baking soda into her coat, gently massage it in, then brush it out.

• If your cat does not like the sound of spray conditioner after her bath, spray the conditioner onto a brush, then take the brush through her hair.

• To help give your cat a bath, place a small window screen across the sink. The screen will give your cat something to cling to and prevent her from having to stand in water.

• If your cat struggles during bath time, check your local pet store for a device that combines a solid base with a wire cage secure enough to hold your pet steady but with openings large enough for you to insert your hands to shampoo and rinse your cat.

• Use pet-cleansing wipes to remove dander and saliva from your cat's coat. The product, made from all-natural ingredients, leaves your cat's coat clean and healthy looking.

• If your cat comes into contact with chewing gum, remove it by rubbing an ice cube on the gum until it hardens and can be pulled out. Then wash the area thoroughly.

• If your cat walks on tar, remove it by rubbing butter or margarine on the tarred area until the tar softens and can be pulled off. Repeat if necessary, then bathe your cat's feet.

• If your cat rubs against oil-based paint, wipe it off immediately with a dry cloth then bathe your cat. If the paint has dried and hardened, cut it out, then bathe your cat. ***Caution: Do not use paint remover, kerosene, turpentine, or gasoline to remove paint from your cat's hair.***

• Never use on your cat shampoo or bathing products that are intended for dogs. Depending on the formula, the product can be toxic to your cat.

Hairy Hair Balls

When a cat washes herself, she ingests loose hair that can become trapped in her stomach. The results of your cat's cleanliness may come back to haunt her when she must hack up a hair ball, without regard to where the gooey mass lands. Although unsightly, hair balls are relatively innocuous most of the time. If your cat appears to be trying to cough one up without success, the hair ball may be lodged somewhere along her digestive system. If the hair ball grows large enough to cause blockage, surgery may be required to remove it. To prevent hair buildup in Pretty's pipes, try some of these suggestions.

- Groom your cat regularly to pick up loose hair.

- Offer a weekly dose of hair ball remedy or pet laxative.

- If your cat will not eat the hair ball remedy, put a dab on her foot so she will lick it off.

- If your cat flings the dab of hair ball remedy you placed on her foot onto the wall or carpet, place a dab on her shoulder where she will be more inclined to lick it off.

- If your cat refuses to open her mouth for the hair ball remedy, put some on your index finger and rub it into the side of her closed mouth.

- Offer your cat an occasional dab of white petroleum jelly instead of hair ball remedy. Because petroleum jelly can interfere with the absorption of nutrients, keep the dab small and offer it only once a week or less.

- Offer your cat a dab of butter instead of hair ball remedy to keep the pipes greased.

- Alternatively, once a week put 1/4 teaspoon (1.2 ml) of cooking oil into your cat's canned food portion.

Pearly Whites

A pretty smile may not be on your cat's priority list, but having sound teeth to chew her food certainly is. Your veterinarian will examine your cat's teeth as part of her annual checkup, but don't wait until a yearly exam to help prevent her from developing dental disease. Tartar and plaque can form on your cat's teeth as they can on your own, and tooth loss and gum disease can just as easily develop. Some cats develop dental problems as they age. Whatever the cause, help your cat in the dental department by cleaning her teeth twice weekly and following some of these suggestions.

• Accustom your cat to having her teeth cleaned early in life. Make the session a game, and reward her with a tartar-control treat.

• Two types of teeth-cleaning products fit over the pet owner's fingertips. One is a rubber device a little larger than a thimble with tiny rubber spikes on it for cleaning your cat's teeth. The other has an actual brush on it so that you can brush your cat's teeth using toothpaste intended for cats. The latter can be sterilized in a microwave oven after each use.

• If you prefer to use an actual brush, use a soft toothbrush for a baby.

• If your cat has a very small mouth, use a woman's eyebrow brush.

• If you use a toothbrush, use toothpaste developed for pets or try a little baking soda instead of pet toothpaste to clean your cat's teeth. *Caution: Never use human toothpaste. Human toothpaste is intended to be spit out and will make your cat sick if she swallows any.*

- Rub your cat's teeth several times a week with a dampened terry cloth. To make it more enjoyable for your cat, moisten the cloth with a little juice from a can of people tuna or sardines.

- Offer your cat treats or food products that are designed to remove plaque and prevent the buildup of tartar.

- Give your cat some hard, dry, crunchy food as a part of her normal diet to help clean plaque deposits.

- Discuss with your veterinarian having your cat's teeth cleaned professionally. Teeth cleaning requires that your cat be anesthetized.

- If your cat has poorly aligned teeth, orthodontic appliances are a possibility. Discuss options with your veterinarian.

- If your cat has bad breath, it could signal disease. Have your cat checked by a veterinarian. To help reduce bad breath, purchase products in pet stores intended to make your cat's breath smell better.

- Mix three parts water to one part non-mint-flavored liquid chlorophyl (available in health food stores) in a medicine bottle. Liquid chlorophyl is a natural deodorant and deodorizes from the inside out. Give your cat one-fourth of a dropper daily to fight bad breath.

Stifling the Stinks

If your cat comes into contact with a skunk, aromatherapy will take on a whole new meaning. If your cat is not allowed to run free, chances are she will never come face-to-face, or face-to-rear, with a skunk. However, if your cat meets one of these cute but smelly creatures head on, here are some remedies for removing the skunk's lingering, musky odor from her coat.

• Wash your cat with tomato juice followed by a bath using pet shampoo and water. Rinse your cat with water and lemon juice or vinegar.

• Try a pet-safe odor neutralizer that can be used to bathe your cat. Read the directions carefully to make certain the product is safe for your cat.

Grooming Resources

Try some of these helpful books before taking the grooming plunge with your pet.

Ballner, Maryjean, "Cat Massage: A Whiskers-to-Tail Guide to Your Cat's Ultimate Petting Experience," St. Martin's Press, 1997.

Buckle, Jane, "How to Massage Your Cat," IDG Books, 1996.

Kohl, Sam, "Cat Grooming Guide," AARONCO, 1997.

If you prefer to see how grooming is done rather than read about it, check out the following video.

For the Love of Animals, "Basics of Cat Grooming," VHS Tape, Tapeworm Video, 1996.

Behavior Tips

Cats, although domesticated for thousands of years, bring with them some of the behaviors found in their wild ancestors. When domestic cats are forced to live in the wild, these behaviors help them survive. In our homes, the same behaviors range from moderately cute to annoying or even dangerous. Behavior problems are one of the major reasons pets are relinquished to shelters or euthanized by veterinarians. Aggression, biting, and urine marking are just a few. If your good efforts cannot solve a behavior problem, enlisting the help of a certified animal behavior consultant may be the next step. See the resources at the end of this chapter for how to find one.

Attack Cat on Duty

Aggression in cats may be associated with fear; establishing, controlling, and protecting territories both inside and outside the home; psychoses; relationships with others of the same species; play; or feeling pain. Cats become aggressive because they feel threatened—whether the threat is real or imagined. They will use the only weapons they have at their disposal—their teeth, claws, and bodies—to ward off the potential danger. Aggressive cats will exhibit a variety of facial expressions, including lowering their ears, staring, crouching, and baring their teeth. Aggressive cats may growl or emit a high-pitched sound from their throats, hiss, or twitch their tails. They may swat and scratch and, in the extreme, attack and bite.

Most animals exhibit some types of aggression periodically. Aggression is one of the ways animals communicate. A certain amount naturally occurs between members of the same species. When the aggression becomes common-place or threatens human members of the house or other pets, the behav-ior is a problem. As with all behavior problems, prevention is the best cure. Even if you live with a mild-mannered wimp, your cat may develop aggressive tenden-cies as a result of environmental factors or her physical condi-tion as she ages.

• If your previously peaceable cat shows signs of aggression, have her examined by a veterinarian to make certain nothing physical is causing her to behave aggressively. Your cat may have a physical problem that causes her to experience pain when you pet or lift her, for example.

• Determine if anything environmental is causing your cat to be aggressive. For example, is anyone in the home teasing your cat? If the source of your cat's aggression is environmental, eliminate what is causing her to react aggressively.

• If you have eliminated physical and environmental conditions as a source of the aggressive behavior, nip the problem in the bud. Whatever technique you use, practice it consistently and immedi-ately. Waiting an hour after your cat has conducted herself aggres-sively won't have any affect.

• Punishment should never be physical. Its intent is to startle the cat and disrupt her behavior.

• Staring is threatening behavior for cats. Avoid staring at your cat, especially if she appears aggressive. When looking at or gazing at your cat, blink slowly every few seconds. Blinking allows mutual gazing without intimidation.

• Do not take chances on being hurt by an aggressive cat. If your cat is threatening, appears dangerous and possibly injurious, consult a professional behaviorist. The behaviorist will outline a plan to correct the behavior based on your cat, the type of aggression, and the source of the problem.

• If your cat becomes aggressive with you, try confining her to one room of the house with all of her necessities. Visit her regularly. Bring food treats every time you visit to make each contact with a person a positive one.

• Some cats may attack their owner's ankles to get attention. Loudly clap your hands and say, "*No*," then redirect a cat's energy to a favorite toy. Interactive toys that require your involvement are a great way to dissipate a cat's pent-up energy.

• Spending regularly scheduled playtime with your cat is the best way to avoid attention-seeking aggression.

• Never play games with your cat that involve using your hands. Your cat will assume that your hand is just another toy and, as a result, attack and bite it the way she would attack a toy.

• If one cat in your household is more aggressive to another one, put a bell onto the more aggressive one's collar to let the other cats know if she is approaching.

• Wear or carry a long rope, clothesline, or string while you are in the home so that you can flick it immediately for your cat to play with if she pounces on you.

• In a multi-cat household, keep the aggressive cat in a confined area, and reintroduce the cats more slowly.

• If one of your cats is aggressive to another one, allow the cats to take turns having free run of the house. Confine one or the other during specified times of the day. Keep the timing consistent so that both cats can become accustomed to the schedule.

- A cat may redirect aggression to a household member or pet if she sees another cat outside. If this occurs, keep the cat away from any windows where she might view the intruder. Ideally, you should find the strange cat's owner or trap her and take her to a shelter. If your cat takes exception to stray cats visiting, don't leave food outside to attract strays.

- If your cat seems stressed at seeing another cat outside, use a piece of cardboard to redirect her to another room where her view will be limited. Do not use your hands to move your cat in order to avoid being attacked, scratched, or bitten.

- If your aggressive cat fights with another cat, use water to separate the two cats.

Biting the Hand That Feeds

You may think the game you are playing with Fluffy is fun, but your cat may think otherwise. As a general rule, animals bite because, from the cat's perspective, the person bitten presented a potential threat or was engaging in conduct that the animal found objectionable. An example is a cat with a low tolerance for being petted biting the hand that is petting her.

- If you are planning to purchase or adopt a cat and you have young children in the house, train the children early how to approach and handle the cat. Cats that are chased, tormented, or teased in what the kids perceive as fun are the ones that are most likely to attack when they have had enough.

- Learn to recognize pre-attack body language and stop interacting with your cat immediately, even if you feel that what you are doing is not offensive. Your cat may think otherwise.

- Do not play aggressive games with your cat. Cats that are petted roughly will soon attack any hand that tries to pet them.

- If your cat nips or bites while you are petting her, your cat may be sensitive to being touched. Signs of impending bites include tail twitching, tensing of the body, turning around quickly, or slightly flattened ears. Do not force the issue—simply pet your cat for shorter periods of time to desensitize her.

Chewing

Does your pet seem to have an oral fixation? Does your cat want to put things into her mouth that she shouldn't? Kittens chew because they are teething. When an owner, family member, or other pet is gone, chewing may become a compulsive behavior due to separation anxiety. If your cat's chewing is gnawing at your nerves, follow some of the suggestions below to curb the crunching.

- Whenever possible, keep objects away from your cat that she finds fun to chew, whether they are needles, pins, or pieces of string or ribbon from packages.

HOW-TO: Identify a Dog-Friendly Cat and Vice Versa

Adopting or purchasing a dog known to get along with cats will save you time and energy helping each adjust to the other. A dog exposed to cats or a cat exposed to dogs some time in the past is more likely to get along with a newcomer brought into the home, assuming the exposure was a positive one. Needless to say, if your cat was chased up a tree by a neighborhood dog, she is going to be hesitant if not fearful of any dog you bring into the house. If you obtained your cat at a shelter, ask the shelter staff if they know anything about her history and whether she came from a home that had dogs. If you purchased your cat from a breeder, inquire what other kinds of pets the breeder has. If you don't know ahead of time, try some of these techniques for identifying a dog-friendly cat.

1. If your cat enjoys the company of visitors and does not hide when the doorbell rings, she is more likely to accept the company of a safe dog than a cat that is skittish and uncomfortable around anyone but you.
2. If your cat appears disinterested when she sees a dog walk by outside your home, she may react positively to a dog that you adopt.
3. Set up a test situation in your home. Cats are more likely to become stressed at the veterinarian's office. Therefore, performing the test at home will make your resident cat feel more secure and give her a place to run and hide if the meeting does not appear successful. Have a friend or neighbor bring in a

• Spray bitter apple onto objects such as electric cords to prevent your cat from sinking her teeth into them.

• Rub favorite objects with scented oils that are unappealing to your cat, such as eucalyptus, cinnamon, or citrus.

• Spray a cologne that is not your scent onto objects to dissuade the chewer.

• If your cat is teething, offer her a variety of chew toys. Direct her attention to them when you observe her chewing something she shouldn't.

• While often thought to be in the purview of dog training, crate or kennel training may be the solution for a cat that chews on objects while her owner is away. Place your cat's belongings, food, water, and litter box into the crate so that your pet will feel secure and not chew up your belongings.

dog known to get along with cats. Keep the dog leashed at all times. Have the person sit with the dog. Allow your cat to investigate the dog while you talk reassuringly to your cat. During the process, do not talk to the dog in order to maintain a neutral stance. Your cat may hiss a bit or even raise her hackles, but if your cat appears aggressive toward the dog or she runs and hides, a successful cat-dog relationship might not develop. If your cat remains curious about the dog, even if she does not get too close to the dog, or if your cat appears indifferent, chances are she will adjust to a dog in your home.

4. *If a dog wants to chase small animals he sees when he is outside or on a walk, he will likely do the same to your cat.*

5. *If a dog enjoys pleasing you and other people, the dog will more likely do well when he is introduced to your cat.*

6. *If the dog understands rudimentary behavioral commands and obeys them, you will have a better chance of establishing a successful relationship with your cat.*

7. *Some of the more aggressive or active breeds of dogs may be a potential hazard to your cat, especially if she is a kitten. A sight hound bred to chase smaller animals may have a difficult time containing himself around a playful kitten.*

- If your cat engages in destructive chewing, especially if the target is a part of your cat's body, she could be bored. Schedule regular play sessions each day so that your cat will anticipate them. Make sure your cat has your complete attention during the play sessions and does not have to share you with the telephone, the television, or other disturbances around the house or around the neighborhood.

Happy to Meet You

If you have a resident cat and want to adopt a dog, the good news is that the two have a great chance of getting along. The bad news is that temperaments of individual animals vary, so see the hints on pages 66–67 to determine if your cat will be receptive to a companion of another ilk.

HOW-TO: Introduce Cats and Dogs

The following guidelines will help your two potential pets get off on the right paw whether you are bringing home a dog to a resident cat or a cat to a resident dog.

1. *Isolate the dog in a separate room for a week or more. If no room is available for the dog, use a crate big enough for the dog. Include food, water, and toys. Put the crate in a private location that is away from the hustle and bustle of the house.*
2. *Spend time interacting with the dog so that he gets to know you and feel comfortable in your presence.*
3. *Spend time with your cat so that she does not feel that she is being abandoned or feel her territory is being invaded by the new dog.*
4. *Do not hurry the introductory process. Your pets will be spending their days together for a long time, so be prepared to spend a few weeks or even months, if necessary, making certain the introductions work.*
5. *Never force the introductions. Do not take a kitten or cat to the resident dog or vice versa. Holding them up to one another before they are ready can cause irreparable harm and prevent the two animals from ever liking each other.*
6. *Give the two animals constant supervision during initial face-to-face meetings. Observe them closely to determine when to give them the space to become better acquainted.*
7. *Allow the animals to have an occasional spat as long as neither is in danger. A dog's playful bark may alarm a cat the first time the cat hears him, but your cat will soon learn what it means. A cat's swat of annoyance at a dog that is overly eager may sting the first time, but the dog will soon learn not to be too gregarious in the cat's presence.*

8. During the introductory process, provide each pet with a place to go that is off-limits to the other so that they can feel comfortable and safe.

9. Prior to face-to-face meetings, rub each of the animals with a towel that has been rubbed over the other to familiarize each with the other's scent.

10. Feed both animals on either side of the door to the room in which the dog is isolated so that they can associate something positive with each other's presence. Placing the dog in a crate is an effective way to allow your resident cat to learn about the dog without having to deal with him personally. Place the crate in the kitchen at mealtimes, and allow the dog to eat when your cat does. Since your cat will be able to observe the dog rather than simply smell him on the other side of a door, do not place the food bowls on either side of the crate. Put the cat's food dish where your cat normally eats so that she can become accustomed to the dog's presence but not intimidated by it.

11. If the dog has not had obedience training, learning the basic commands of sit, stay, come, and no would be a good approach before allowing the dog to meet the cat.

12. Once the dog learns to identify the cat as a normal component of the home, begin allowing the dog to meet the cat nose to nose. Keep the dog leashed, and allow the cat to come to the dog. Talk to both in a calm voice. Offer both of them treats.

13. If the new dog is interested but not aggressive, allow him to examine your cat. If the dog appears too eager, give the leash a gentle tug and command your dog to sit or stay. Continue allowing both pets to meet on a limited basis until you are confident that the dog will accept your cat.

Nocturnal Commotions

Face it, being with her human companion is one of your cat's favorite pastimes. Whether you are reading a book, watching television, gardening, or working on the computer, your cat will want to participate in what you are doing. Unfortunately, when you sleep, your cat may find other, more noisy ways to occupy her time. Cats are basically nocturnal, so you may find yourself being awakened in the wee hours of the morning whether you want to be or not. If you are having trouble getting some shut-eye, try some of these suggestions to suppress your cat's nighttime crazies before they drive you berserk.

• Have your cat examined by a veterinarian to make sure the nighttime serenade is not due to an illness or physical discomfort.

• Feed your cat just before bedtime. Be firm about not giving in to your cat's begging for earlier meals in addition to her later one to prevent her from becoming overweight.

• Play vigorously with your cat for 15 minutes before bedtime.

• To keep your cat out of the bedroom at night, confine her to a room of the house in which you put a set of her belongings—food and water dishes, toys, and a litter box.

• Give your cat about 1/8 teaspoon (0.6 ml) of loose chamomile tea as a moist treat before bedtime, or chill some chamomile tea and put it into her water dish.

• As a last resort, discuss with your veterinarian the possibility of using drug therapy if your cat is hyperactive during the night.

• Provide your cat with a window perch so she can watch the world during the wee hours.

Obeying Your Commands

Imagine if you or another household member held a door open too long and your cat, seeing an opportunity for an escapade, escaped before you had a chance to stop her. Or, remember when you spent an hour crawling under the furniture the last time you had to get your cat into her carrier. These and a thousand other scenarios are good reasons to give your cat the rudiments of obedience training. If you teach your cat the commands *sit, stay, come,* and *down,* you may prevent an accident from befalling her and reduce the stress both of you feel when she doesn't listen to you. Once your cat has mastered the basics, the sky's the limit for teaching her lots of other instructions or tricks.

One of the hottest training methods these days uses a nifty, ingenious gadget called a clicker. A clicker is a small metal device or child's cricket that has a piece of spring steel attached that makes a clicking sound when pressed. If initially accompanied by a positive reinforcement, such as food, clickers reinforce the reward during training until the sound of the clicker itself becomes the reinforcer for good behavior. Such associations are called secondary reinforcement and have been used in animal training for many years. They are even in use in your home now. When you operate the can opener, your cat comes running because she assumes that food will follow. The sound of the can opener acts as reinforcement for a desired activity. In the same way, the sound of the clicker acts as reinforcement because your cat will associate it with a primary reward stimulus, such as food. You will find basic instructions for clicker training on the next page.

Potty Training

Once cats are trained by their mothers how to urinate and defecate, they do it constantly. Even though your cat will determine when she relieves herself, where she does so is your choice. Training a cat to use the litter box is often as simple as showing her where it is. Cats love to dig, so providing a box with digging material of some type may be all you need.

• To encourage your new cat or kitten to use her box, ask for some used litter to bring with you from the shelter or breeder where you obtained her. Place the used litter into the new box so that she will be familiar with the scent.

• Confining your new kitten or cat in a comfortable room for her first week or two in your home will accustom her to using the litter box. Place the litter box in a visible area of the room so that she can see when you or other family members approach. When the time has come to move the litter box to a more desirable location, move the box a few feet (meters) at a time so that your cat always knows where the box is.

HOW-TO: Clicker Train Your Cat

Before beginning to teach basic commands, set up your sessions by following these steps.

1. *Before beginning to train your cat, make the clicking sound when you feed her regular meals or when you offer her a treat so she begins to associate the sound with eating. After you have done this for a week or so, go to her regular feeding station and make the clicking sound. If she comes running, she has associated the sound of the clicker with being fed. Now you can begin the specific training. Offer food on this occasion so she continues to make the connection.*

2. *If you are not in a good mood, your cat will pick up on your negative emotions and associate them with the commands, resulting in less inclination to obey them.*

3. *Keep sessions about 10 or 15 minutes in length to keep your cat from becoming bored or frustrated.*

4. *Do not use a word or phrase for a command during one session and use a different one during the next session for the same activity. Changing your commands will only confuse your cat. Keep the commands to one or two words.*

5. *Select as the food reward something that is extra appealing to your cat.*

6. *Conduct training sessions prior to regular meals so that your cat is hungry and more apt to perform for the food reward. Don't starve her to train her, however.*

7. *Train your cat in a location that is free of distractions, and give the process your complete attention. Watching your favorite television show may be a good time to use the exercycle but not a good time to train your cat.*

8. *Use your cat's name along with the command you are trying to teach. In addition to the food reward, praise her when she performs the behavior you desire.*

9. *Always have your clicker and food reward on hand when you begin your session. If you cannot obtain a clicker, use another device such as a small plastic container of treats that you rattle, two spoons that you click together, or even clucking your tongue, but be consistent. Starting with one device then changing to another later on means you will have to start training from the beginning.*

10. *Always click at the moment your cat is performing the behavior you want.*

- If you would like to use a different kind of litter than what your cat used before you adopted or purchased her, mix the new litter in with the brand your cat is accustomed to. Gradually increase the quantity of the preferred brand until you have switched over completely.

- If your cat has to compete with traffic in and out of the house, must pass Fido's bed to get to the box, or must walk across a damp basement floor to do her business, you may find her relieving herself elsewhere. Make sure your cat's box is in a private, easily accessible location.

Sit

1. With your cat facing you, let her smell the food, then slowly move the food reward back and over her head. As her head follows the food, she will naturally sit down. Make the clicking sound, and offer her the food reward immediately. Continue the process. When your cat sits, make the clicking sound and give her the food immediately.
2. Once your cat learns the behavior, give it a name, such as sit. Say "Sit." Soon she will begin to associate the food reward with the command, and you will no longer have to use the clicker to make her sit. Saying "Sit" will be enough.
3. Some animal trainers suggest that you place a cat on a table or stool to conduct the sessions. Just be careful what you use does not confuse your cat into thinking jumping onto surfaces that you may not want her to jump onto is all right.

Come

1. Now that you have already trained your cat to come to her food bowl at the sound of the clicker, you can begin to associate the command come with the behavior. Say your cat's name, hit the clicker, and say "Come."
2. When your cat comes to the food station, offer a treat. Try using the same technique from other locations around the house. When she comes, hit the clicker a few times and praise her. Give your cat the food reward immediately. Gradually, just say "Come" to call your cat.

You can use these same techniques to get your cat to learn other commands like down or stay.

Scaredy-cats

Four-legged animals are as inclined to experience stress as much as their two-legged owners. While your cat won't labor over where her next meal might come from, she may wrestle with her own fears and anxieties. Fear may be associated with a particular person, a gender, or a specific situation, such as riding in the car or visiting the veterinarian's office. Cats may become anxious when they hear certain noises such as thunder or fireworks, when a new pet enters the house, or when an animal companion dies. Eliminating the cause is the first step in preventing your cat's anxiety attacks. If your cat runs under the bed when a thunderstorm approaches, the source of the stress is clear. Sometimes the cause of the stress is more difficult to determine. To help a nervous cat, try some of these tension-taming tips.

• If your cat has a fear of thunder or fireworks, desensitizing her is almost impossible. Instead, provide a place in your home away

from windows and doors in which your cat can stay and wait out the storm.

• Keep a radio on to help drown out the sounds of thunder or fireworks.

• If your cat experiences anxiety over a new pet addition to the home, separate them and reintroduce the animals gradually.

• If your cat becomes stressed because you are moving to a new home, take your cat to your new home, if possible, and allow her to investigate the surroundings before you move in. Give your cat some treats or play with her in the new home so she will associate something positive with the experience.

- If a new baby or new spouse is making your cat anxious, try to keep things as normal as possible. Stick to your cat's regular schedule, and provide her with plenty of attention to let her know that she is not being replaced.

- If your cat exhibits grieving behavior due to the loss of an animal companion, provide her with plenty of love and affection. After you both heal, consider adopting a new animal playmate.

- If necessary, consult with a veterinary or animal behaviorist to help solve your cat's anxiety.

- If your cat develops severe anxieties that cannot be solved with behavior modification techniques, discuss drug options with your veterinarian. Calming drugs may be the only way to help some animals overcome their anxieties.

- The word scaredy-cat didn't develop without reason. Many cats fear strangers, so allowing your cat the option of hiding when a visitor arrives is the best solution to controlling her anxieties. When your cat learns to trust your guests, she will make their acquaintance.

Sniff and Scratch

Even though you give your cat a regular pedicure, she still views your furniture and belongings as her own personal emery board. Clawing is a very natural and instinctive feline behavior and, apparently, lots of fun. Outdoors, scratching is completely appropriate. Inside your home, however, it is one of the destructive feline behaviors you want to displace.

- The best way to discourage clawing of inappropriate objects is to provide your cat with something of her own to claw. Scratching posts come in a variety of styles and sizes to satisfy the natural urges of every feline. Some cats prefer to scratch carpet, while others enjoy clawing wood, sisal rope, or other materials. The best scratching post for your cat is one that combines several clawing media and has multiple levels on which your cat can exercise her body and her rights. Encourage your cat to use her post by rubbing some catnip onto the post. When you see your cat using it, praise her profusely. Offer treats to your cat and to yourself for a job well done.

• To keep your cat from clawing the corners of your upholstered furniture, attach ready-made corners.

• Cover the corners of your upholstered furniture with aluminum foil to foil the clawing kitty.

• There are products available that will keep Kitty away from your upholstered furnishings—nontoxic plastic strips that you apply directly to your chairs, sofas, and anything else you don't want your cat to sink her claws into.

• Place double-sided sticky tape onto the corners of your furniture.

• Tape a paper bag onto the corners of your upholstered furniture.

• Cut and attach a plastic rug runner knobby-side up to the corners of upholstered furniture.

• Declawing, although common, can be traumatic and painful. Instead of declawing your cat, try buying little caps that fit over your cat's nails. They are easy to apply and last about six weeks before needing replacement. They even come in colors for the fashion-conscious kitty. Ask your veterinarian or check in your local pet store.

• Spray a little lemon juice, cinnamon oil, or eucalyptus oil onto the corners of your upholstered furniture. Pre-test an area of the fabric to make sure the oil doesn't discolor it.

- If your cat scratches your wood furniture or your kitchen cabinets, rub the corners with cinnamon, eucalyptus, or lemon oil.

- Wrap a piece of carpet around the corners of cabinets or paneled walls so your cat can scratch the carpet rather than the wood.

- Place a small, freestanding scratch post in front of your cat's favorite scratching spot.

- Instead of replacing your furniture, cover it with an attractive quilt or throw. Doing so is much cheaper than reupholstering.

Furniture alternatives to dissuade clawing

- If your cat will not leave your upholstered furniture alone and continues to claw it in spite of all your best efforts, replace it with furniture that is not attractive to your cat, such as a futon, other wood-framed furniture, or rattan with comfy cushions.

- Fabrics that dissuade a clawing or chewing cat are smooth ones such as satin, leather, faux leather, velour, or velvet. Avoid heavy woven fabrics that draw your cat like a magnet.

Taming Tensions

Put two or more people under the same roof, and tensions occasionally flare up. If two people can't always keep the lid on emotional outbreaks, why should cats be expected to? Naturally, your cats will have spats periodically. After all, they are often the only ones that know what circumstances brought about the disagreement. If the cats appear to be in danger from one another, breaking up the brawl may be necessary. If your feline housemates get into a squabble, try some of these methods to separate them without risking your own life or limbs.

• Reproductive drives can be a source of fighting, especially among males. Therefore, spaying or neutering your cats will reduce outbreaks that result from biological urges.

• Proper introductions and training will go a long way in preventing fights before they start. For details on how to introduce cats, see the section called "Happy to Meet You" in this chapter.

• Water is one of the most effective and most harmless ways to separate two cats that have locked horns. If the animals are outside, squirt them with a hose. If indoors, squirt them with a squirt bottle, or grab the nearest plastic container and fill it with water to douse the two.

• Give your cats their own food dishes, beds, and toys to discourage competition, which may cause them to fight.

Up, Up, and Away

Getting up and away to observe the world below seems to be the favorite feline pastime, second only to eating, sleeping, and sitting on anything you are trying to read. You may decide that your cat can go where she pleases. However, if you determine that certain spots are off-limits to your flying feline, try some of these suggestions to keep her from defying gravity.

• Spray your kitchen countertops with ARMORALL, which makes the countertops so slick that your cat will not want to jump onto them.

• Spray off-limit surfaces with a kitty repellent that you can purchase in pet stores. The repellent has an offensive odor that will keep your cat from wanting to jump to a specific location. Pre-test a small area to make sure the repellent won't stain or discolor the surface.

- Place small pots filled with eucalyptus, cinnamon, or citrus pot-pourri at locations where your cat likes to jump. The odor might be enough to dissuade your high-flying feline.

- Feed your cat before you prepare your own meal to keep Kitty from wanting to get onto your kitchen counters while you are fixing dinner.

- Place a plastic rug runner, knobby-side up, on your countertops when you're not at home. The plastic bumps are uncomfortable, and your cat will not want to walk on them.

"Urine" My Territory

Meowing, purring, and cater-wauling are just a few of the ways a cat will let you or another animal know how she feels. Reading a cat's mind can be as easy as reading her body language. Therefore, knowing the meaning of signals such as tail twitching, teeth baring, or head butting is an important step to understanding what your cat is telling you. One of the ways cats communicate with other cats is by scent marking. Unless the marker carries with it a powerful odor, such as a male cat's urine spray, you may never fathom the subtleties of communication by scent. Scent markers provide some geographic orientation for a cat so that she can identify the space as being inhabited by another. If the cat is lost, scent markers help her find her way home. Scent marking also helps an animal be more comfortable and self-assured about where she is. Lastly, cats may engage in allo-marking—marking other members of the group—to give them a common smell for the purposes of identification. When a cat scent marks her owner, she says, "You are an accepted member of my feline family."

Scent marking is a natural behavior. Scent marks can result when a cat rubs against an object or when she claws or digs. The most common form of scent marking, however, is achieved when a cat sprays urine. Although spraying to mark territory is a behavior commonly associated with male cats, females also spray. A cat will sniff, then back up to a vertical surface, quiver her tail, and squirt urine. Cats leave these scent markers for any future feline travelers to smell. Inside your home, cats also may scent mark territories. Even the presence of cats outside the home may elicit the urine-marking behavior from the indoor pet.

• The best way to stop urine marking before it starts is to have your cat neutered or spayed. Urine marking is prevalent among sexually intact and active cats, so altering will help remove the drive. Veterinarians are spaying and neutering cats at an earlier age, so discuss the possibility of altering your cat soon after you adopt her.

• Drug therapy may help a spraying cat, particularly if she dribbles or marks due to fears and anxieties. Eliminating the source of the anxiety is the first step in solving the problem. However, you may want to discuss drug alternatives with your veterinarian if a behavior modification program does not work.

• Change the function of the marked spot by placing your cat's food bowls at the location.

• If a particular spot in your home is attractive to your cat, keep her away from the area altogether.

Behavior Resources

For further reading, try some of these general books about cat behavior.

Dodman, Nicholas H., "The Cat Who Cried for Help: Attitudes, Emotions, and the Psychology of Cats," Bantam Doubleday Dell Publishers, 1997.

Lachman, Larry, and Frank Mickadeit, "Cats on the Counter," Overlook Press, 2000.

Maggitti, Phil, "Guide to a Well-Behaved Cat," Barron's Educational Series, Inc., 1993.

Shojai, Amy, "Competability: A Practical Guide to Building a Peaceable Kingdom Between Cats and Dogs," Three Rivers Press, 1998.

To teach children pet safety, try the video "Dogs, Cats and Kids," Pet Partnerships, P.O. Box 11331, Chicago, IL 60611-0331, 1-800-784-0979.

To find a certified applied animal behaviorist, visit the Animal Behavior Society's Web page at *www.cisab.indiana.edu/ABS/Applied/index.html* for the most up-to-date listing.

Check out these other commercial Web sites about clicker training.

www.ClickerTrain.com/
www.clickandtreat.com/

Clicker-training material also can be ordered on-line from *www.amazon.com/*.

Seasonal Tips

This chapter includes survival tips that follow your cat through the seasons of the year and the seasons of her life. Included are tips for battling the heat and cold, helping cats that have access to the outdoors, traveling with your cat, and, finally, saying good-bye.

Cool Cats

The dog days of summer have special meaning for your cat. Warm weather brings a host of problems for cats whose furry coats hold the heat. Because cats have no sweat glands distributed throughout their bodies, they are more susceptible to heat-related discomforts and must rely on panting or sweating via their footpads as a way to deal with the heat and humidity. Like you, your cat will appreciate some help battling hot or humid weather.

- Air-conditioning is the best way to help your cat stay cool in the warm weather. However, if you don't have that luxury, place fans in places where your cat likes to sleep. Window fans on exhaust will help circulate the air inside your home and keep your pet from heating up.

- Allow your cat access to cooler rooms of the house, such as the basement, the garage, or a screened porch with a nice breeze.

- Keep your cat's water dish filled with fresh, cool water. Place ice cubes in the water during the hottest periods of the day.

- Older and overweight cats are more at risk from the heat, so be more sensitive to them in warm weather.

- To prevent heat exhaustion, don't ever leave your cat in a closed car.

- Tether your cat outside only under your supervision. Provide plenty of shade for her.

HOW-TO: Recognize Heat Stress

Heat-related problems in cats include heat exhaustion (from prolonged exposure to intense heat) or heatstroke (from exposure to high temperatures and humidity). Cats suffering from heat stresses may suffer cellular breakdown, brain damage, and heart failure, resulting in death. If your cat is elderly, over-weight, suffers from cardiovascular or respiratory problems, or is one of the short-nosed breeds, she could be more susceptible to heat-related stresses. The symptoms listed below could signal danger.

Anxious expression
Dazed or unconscious
Heavy panting
High fever (above 104° Fahrenheit (40°C))
Lethargy, fatigue
Pawing at doors or kennel openings
Salivation
Staggering
Vomiting, diarrhea
Warm, dry skin
Weakness

If you suspect your cat is suffering from heat exhaustion or heatstroke, reduce her temperature by immersing her in a tub or container of tepid water or water her down with wet towels. Do not use ice or ice water because the extremely cold temperature of the ice could cause shock. Take her to a veterinarian immediately.

Gardening with Cats in Mind

Outdoors, your cat may enjoy digging up your geraniums or depositing wastes onto your watermelons. Your cat may find digging the dirt from your houseplants and depositing it onto the floor for later use to be fun. If you notice cats that are not your own entering your yard or digging up your garden, try to find out whose cats they are. Discuss with the owners about keeping them indoors or leashed. Many communities have leash laws for cats, so you may have legal muscle to back up your friendly discussions. If the cats don't belong to anyone, refer to the section in this chapter about rescuing free-roaming animals. To keep your cat from starting her own landscaping business, try some of these tips for turning your four-legged dirt-devil into a lawn lover.

• Check at farm or garden stores for chemical products developed to repel cats from choosing your garden as a favorite place to deposit wastes. The odor is designed to stop animals from leaving their droppings around your home.

• Sprinkle alum powder around bushes or objects in your garden your cat likes to dig up.

• To keep cats from digging in your outdoor garden, sprinkle the garden with moth crystals. If you have kids, cover the moth crystals with dirt.

• Insert evergreen cones into the dirt of your potted plants, or cover the dirt with lemon or orange peels. Or, place aluminum foil over the pot.

• Bury a cotton ball dipped in oil of cloves just below the surface of the soil.

• If you use a chemical lawn treatment, insecticide, or fertilizer, make sure your cat stays off of it for the specified amount of time (usually 24 hours), depending on the product you use.

- If you have used a lawn flea treatment, keep your cat off the lawn until it is safe. Read the product label directions to determine how long your cat should keep off the grass.

- To keep a cat from using the garden as an outdoor litter box, plant ground cover around shrubs, trees, and other plants. If she cannot get to the dirt to dig, she will go elsewhere.

- An alternative way to keep cats from digging in your garden is to spread lemon or orange peels around. Most cats do not care for the citrus smell.

- To prevent your cat from climbing a tree in your yard, give the tree an Elizabethan-style collar, which can be made of screening, wire mesh, or chicken wire.

Old Man Winter

Snowflakes that fall on your nose and eyelashes may be a few of Julie Andrews' favorite things, but your cat may think otherwise. If left outside for extended periods of time, your cat can experience frostbite or hypothermia. To determine if your cat has frostbite, look for discoloring of the skin, especially on the ear tips and other extremities. If you find any, contact your veterinarian. Ice-melting chemicals or antifreeze can be life-threatening for the cat that ingests them. Road salt also can cause sores if it becomes lodged between your cat's foot pads. To help your cat fight the cold, follow these safety precautions and helpful hints.

- Place a flannel sheet over your cat's bed to help her generate heat.

- Floor heating vents can catch identification tags that are attached to your cat's collar. If your cat likes to snooze over a floor vent, make sure she is wearing a breakaway or elastic collar.

- Offer your cat additional food in the winter because she will need extra calories to fight the cold.

- Wipe off your cat's paws when she comes in from the outside to prevent salt and other chemicals from sticking to her feet.

- Keep antifreeze out of your cat's reach, and clean up any that has spilled in the garage or driveway.

- If your cat is accustomed to living the good life indoors, don't allow her to stay outside for extended periods of time in cold weather.

- Since warm air rises, offering your cat a soft bed off the floor will add extra warmth and comfort for winter dreaming.

- If your cat stays outside, provide her with a warm shelter. A winterized doghouse will work just as well for a cat as it will for a dog. Position it off the ground and out of the wind.

- If you prefer not to have a doghouse for your outdoor cat, consider placing a cardboard box inside of a heavy-duty plastic yard or garbage bag, tape down the edges inside the box, and raise the bottom flap to provide some shelter from the wind. Set the box up off the ground, place it close to and facing your house, and fill with some straw or carpet for extra warmth. Anchor it down with a board on the top.

- Bang on your car's hood or blow the horn before starting the engine to make sure that no cats are sleeping inside to keep warm.

Outdoor Access

Outdoor access can be safe if your cat goes from the house into an enclosure. Cats should not be allowed to roam freely outside for their own protection and the protection of neighbors and property. If you allow your cat access to a fenced-in yard or enclosure, follow some of these suggestions to make life easier for both of you.

- Check the classifieds in the major pet magazines or the catalogs listed in the last chapter for prefabricated or standardized enclosures or pens.

- Place a grass mat inside at your cat's pet door to prevent her from tracking mud inside the house.

- A plastic carpet runner leading from your cat's door will protect carpet from muddy pet footprints.

- If your cat goes into an outdoor enclosure at will, keep her confined to the room into which the pet door opens until you have an opportunity to wash her feet and check for fleas and ticks.

- If you want to give your cat some outdoor exposure, train her to be comfortable on a leash. Put a harness on your cat while she is indoors for about ten minutes a day for several days. Increase the time she wears her harness to about one hour per day. When she is comfortable in the harness, attach a leash. Bring her outside for short jaunts, gradually increasing the length of time she accompanies you.

- A harness rather than a collar is safer for walking or tethering a cat because harnesses are more difficult to slip out of.

- If you have a fenced yard, consider a fencing-in system that fits on top of your fence to keep your cat from jumping over. The system should fit wooden, chain-link, masonry, or wire fences.

- Build an enclosure for your cat that includes safe plants and climbing trees.

- Pet doors can be installed in windows without cutting holes in your walls. Check the classifieds in the cat magazines or your local hardware store.

- A window extension will allow your cat to view the outside world from a window in your home. Such extensions are similar to window greenhouses and can be sized to fit your windows.

- If you live in an apartment and have a deck or open porch, make it into a safe cat enclosure by attaching screen, chicken wire, wire mesh, or latticework around the railings. Make certain your landlord approves before modifying the structure.

- If you are concerned about your cat jumping over the railing of your apartment deck or porch, buy a doggie-sized crate and install it on the deck. Allow your cat to sit safely outside during the day or evening. Cover the top of the crate to give your cat shade.

Rescuing Free-Roaming Cats

If a cat begins hanging around your house and you cannot find her owner, chances are the animal is a stray. The life of a stray cat is not a pleasant one. Strays are at risk from other animals, cars, uncaring or abusive humans, contagious diseases, and other events that can cause them pain and suffering and bring their lives to an untimely end. By rescuing a stray, you will be saving a life and helping reduce animal overpopulation. Even if the outcome is to take the stray to a shelter, she will have some hope of finding a home.

HOW-TO: Trap a Free-Roaming Cat

Not all stray cats go eagerly with their human saviors. Therefore, arming yourself with some information and ingenuity may be the only way to convince a stray that life with you will be better than life on the streets. If you decide to pursue capturing that stray cat, be cautious and do not risk being injured. Stray or injured animals may be stressed and frightened. Your attempt to help may cause them to behave unpredictably or react defensively to what they consider a potential threat. **Caution: If you have other cats, be sure to isolate the stray until you can have the stray examined by a veterinarian and tested for parasites and contagious diseases.**

Previously owned cats may come to you more easily than ferals—domestic cats born in the wild. Stealth and a bit of trickery may be necessary to capture a feral cat. Feral and stray cats are often guided by their sense of hunger. By using food, those who want to rescue them are apt either to win the cat's trust or to force her capture.

1. Establish a pattern of feeding. Cats are creatures of habit and will catch on quickly.
2. Obtain a humane trap. Contact a local animal organization to determine if it has any available to lend. If you cannot find a humane trap locally, contact Alley Cat Allies, a nonprofit organization promoting non-

lethal feral cat population control. Alley Cat Allies has fact sheets about trapping, obtaining traps, and other feral cat rescue topics.

3. *Set the trap on day seven or eight of the routine feeding. Place it in the same spot where you have been leaving the food. Disguise it with leaves if it is in a wooded area.*

4. *Stay out of sight, but continue to monitor the trap every 15 minutes or so.*

5. *Once the cat is inside, cover the trap with a towel or blanket to help calm her.*

6. *Make plans with a veterinarian to examine the cat immediately. Do not handle her until she is anesthetized.*

7. *If the cat is still wild and not easily handled, place her into a large dog crate, feed and care for her until she is accustomed to you. Free-roaming cats are often considered strays even though they may belong to someone. If you have trapped a stray cat, try to find her owner before making the cat your own.*

8. *For more information about trapping or feral cats in general, contact Alley Cat Allies.*

Static Electricity

Have you ever stooped to touch your cat and seen a spark fly or felt a jolt as your fingers made contact with her hair? During the winter, when the air inside your home is dry, you may experience a slight charge from the buildup of static electricity when you pet your cat. Although the charge is enough to give you and your cat a shock, it is not enough to cause damage to you or your feline companion. If static electricity is giving you static, you can eliminate it with some of these ideas.

• Use a humidifier to add moisture to the air.

• Set basins of water throughout the house to add moisture to the air if you don't have a humidifier.

• Use an antistatic product on your carpet. Spray it on, but be sure to allow it to dry before letting your cat walk on it.

• You can help eliminate static buildup on your cat by using pet cleansing wipes that add moisture to her coat.

• To help control static when you touch your cat, use an antistatic product in the clothes dryer.

• Try a pet moisturizing spray to help eliminate dry skin as a way to control static buildup.

• Wipe your cat's hair with an antistatic dryer sheet.

Traveling with Your Cat

In this time of change, mobility is the operative word for the modern world. On some occasions, our travels are just around the corner. On others, our trips are across town or across the country. Whether we are moving, vacationing, or simply taking a cat to the vet, traveling with our cats is certain to occur sooner or later. Here are some suggestions for making the trip a pleasant one.

Traveling by land

Sharing the company of your favorite feline companion on the road can add an extra measure of merriment to your excursions. Follow these 15 suggestions for making a car trip more enjoyable for both you and your cat.

• Before committing to taking your cat along with you on a vacation, think about how much she will enjoy the trip. Most cats tend to be creatures of habit and may not enjoy cruising the open road. Your cat may cry or whine during the entire trip, making you as miserable as she is. If you are planning a vacation and you think your cat might prefer to stay home, consider leaving your unhappy camper in the care of a professional pet sitter or someone else you trust.

• New experiences, smells, locations, and people can cause stress to even the most intrepid pet traveler. Your cat might develop diarrhea, vomit, pant excessively, or drool. To minimize stress, keep everything as normal as possible. On the trip, give your cat the same food and water to which she is accustomed.

• Make certain that your cat's vaccinations and shots are up-to-date, and carry vaccination certificates and veterinary information with you. If you cross an international border, board your cat during the trip, or seek veterinary medical help, you may be required to show proof of vaccinations. Take along your veterinarian's phone number and any medications your cat might need.

• Take a cat care pack that includes her regular food, a bowl and heavy water dish that will not tip over, a supply of water, an emergency kit, extra blankets, some toys, grooming tools, paper towels, and a litter box and litter. If you are traveling in warm weather, take an ice pack to place into the cat's carrier. For a nontipping dish, check your local automotive supply store for large cup holders with sandbag bottoms, or purchase a nonspill pet dish designed for that purpose.

- Do not feed your cat for about three hours before beginning your trip. If you like, offer your cat a snack while riding, but don't provide dinner until you arrive at your destination.

- Make certain your cat is wearing a collar with identification tags. If she escapes without these tags, you may never find her again. Take along a photo of your cat in case you get separated.

- If your cat suffers from car sickness, discuss medication options with your veterinarian.

- Do not leave your cat in a parked automobile. The inside of the vehicle can reach 120° Fahrenheit (49°C) or more very quickly during the day in warm months. Even venting the window is not enough to provide circulating air. If you must make a rest stop, make it brief and park in the shade.

- If you don't have air-conditioning in your vehicle, travel at night or during cooler times of the day.

- Keep your cat in a carrier or crate at all times. Secure the carrier with a seat belt or other device. A cat allowed to roam in the car while you are driving might decide to rest under the brake pedal or on the dashboard. If you roll down the window, your cat could escape. A mesh carrier will expand to allow your cat to move around while traveling and provides adequate air circulation.

- Make frequent rest stops so your cat can relieve herself or have a drink of water.

- If your trip requires overnight accommodations, know ahead of time which hotels accept pets. Make reservations, and let them know you will be bringing an animal. If you are camping, make certain the campsite or RV park allows pets.

- Take some used litter, and sprinkle a little into your cat's carrier litter box to make her feel at home.

- If you have trouble getting your cat into a carrier, try one of the carriers that has an opening in the top so you can simply lower your cat into it.

• Put a harness on your feline travel companion rather than a collar. Harnesses are more difficult to slip out of.

Traveling by air

Sometimes flying is the best way to travel. Doing so may involve taking your cat on board an airplane or shipping her ahead. Thousands of pets are transported by air every year. However, when the occasional pet succumbs to an airline mishap during transport, it makes headlines. Horror stories abound about pets shipped in too hot or too cold cargo containers and, as a result, have either suffocated or frozen to death. Airline awareness about travel for pets has improved in recent years, though. Follow these guidelines to minimize risks.

• Contact the airline in advance to determine their pet regulations. Try to book a direct flight or one with a minimum number of stops. Travel on the same flight as your cat, and ask to see her being loaded into the cargo hold. If possible, fly during the cool parts of the day in warm weather and warm parts of the day in cool weather.

• Investigate an airline's pet transport policies and procedures before buying your cat a ticket. Is the cargo hold climate controlled? How long will your cat have to wait before she is brought off the airplane at its destination? What other types of cargo will be shipped on your flight? Will someone hand deliver your cat, or will she be whisked into the airport along with the luggage?

• You may be able to take your cat on board with you as long as she is in a carrier that fits under the seat in front of you. Contact the airlines to determine if this method of transport is allowed and for the accepted crate size.

• The Humane Society of the United States recommends not shipping short-nosed cats, such as Persians or Exotic Shorthair cats, in airplane cargo holds. Because of their shortened nasal passages, these breeds are more vulnerable to oxygen deprivation and heatstroke.

- If your cat is to be shipped in the cargo hold, purchase a sturdy carrier approved by the United States Department of Agriculture in which she can stand up and move around. The carrier should have adequate ventilation, and the words *Live Animals* should appear on the top of the crate. Close the crate securely,

HOW-TO: Find a Pet Sitter

If you would prefer to leave Fluffy in the comfort of her own home while you are on a trip, hire a professional pet sitter to care for her while you are away. Having a professional pet sitter care for your cat will prevent her from being stressed due to being transported and will reduce the health risk of being around strange animals. A pet sitter will feed, water, and play with your cat, water your plants, bring in the newspaper and mail, turn lights on and off, feed the fish, and give your home a lived-in look.

1. *Begin the process of finding a pet sitter well in advance of your trip. Pet sitters, like boarding kennels, are booked early, especially over the holidays or during prime vacation time.*

2. *Ask your veterinarian or pet-owning friends for a referral. Finding a sitter who is trustworthy and has a good reputation is important for your peace of mind.*

3. *If you cannot get a referral, check the Yellow Pages of your telephone directory under Pet Sitters. Call several, and set up appointments to interview them. Or, call the locator lines of the two major professional pet-sitting organizations for a list of member pet sitters in your area.*

4. *Ask the pet sitter if she or he is bonded and insured and can supply references. Ask the pet sitter how long he or she has been in business and what experience with animals the person has beyond pet sitting.*

5. *Set up a meeting with the pet sitter so that you and your cat can meet her. The sitter should be interested in your cat and attempt to establish a rapport during the first meeting. Getting to know a cat sometimes takes a while if she is shy, but the sitter should make the effort.*

6. *Expect the sitter to ask you questions about your cat's care including feeding, cleaning up, disposing of wastes, recycling food cans, and games your cat likes to play.*

7. *When you decide on a sitter, expect to sign a contract covering the terms of the sitting, including dates of coverage, cost, and liabilities. Some sitters, like housekeepers, require payment up front, so don't be put off at a sitter asking for payment in advance. When you sign the contract, you will need to give the sitter the key. Decide at that time if you want the sitter to leave the key in your home on the last visit or keep the key until you return. If no one else has a key to your home, allowing the sitter to keep the key until you have returned from your trip may be safer for your cat.*

but don't lock it in case airport personnel must open it in an emergency.

• Fit your cat with identification tags that have your name, address, and phone number as well as the address and phone number of your destination. Carry a photo of your cat in case she is lost.

• Know what, if any, quarantine requirements might be in effect at your travel destination. The state of Hawaii requires that incoming

8. Be sure to let the sitter know of any illnesses or idiosyncracies that your cat has so that the sitter is not surprised if she behaves in a particular way. For example, does your cat get easily fatigued or does she hide from strangers? Even if your cat hides, a sitter should make certain that he or she sees the cat on every visit to know that she is OK. That may mean crawling around and looking under furniture or doing whatever is necessary to find your cat.

9. If your cat eats little while you are gone, let the sitter know and offer suggestions about what to do if she decides to go on a hunger strike. If you free-feed your cat, ask the sitter to measure each meal to determine whether your cat is eating it.

10. Provide the sitter with important information such as the phone number of where you will be, anyone locally to notify in an emergency, and the name and number of your veterinarian.

11. Have your veterinarian keep a letter on file from you that says you are going away and names the pet sitter and service as temporary guardian of your cat. If a problem arises, the sitter will have the authority to seek treatment for your cat, and you will be responsible for any fees.

12. The sitter should give you a business card to take with you so that you can call the sitter if you need to for any reason. If your return is going to be delayed, contact the sitter to take care of your cat for the additional time you will be away.

13. Contact the sitter when you return to let her or him know you are back.

pets be quarantined for four months. The countries comprising Great Britain have a six-month quarantine. If you are planning a two-week jaunt to either of these locations or other ones that will force your cat to spend her time in a cage to see what diseases might develop, don't bother taking her along. If you are moving to a place that requires your cat be quarantined, investigate the quarantine facilities first.

• Take the necessary vaccination certificates with you.

• Do not feed your cat or give her water less than four hours before the flight, and don't tranquilize her before flying.

• Once at your destination, have your cat checked by a veterinarian to make certain she has arrived in good health and withstood the stress of the trip.

Waging War on Allergies (Your Own)

Does the presence of your cat cause you to sneeze unmercifully? Do your eyes fill with tears of misery instead of tears of joy when she wants to be close? Many of us who love animals find that we cannot even pet them without the ahhs becoming the ahh-choos! Pet allergies can cause watery eyes, nasal congestion and runny nose, sneezing, scratchy, sore throat, coughing, wheezing, and even hives. The source of allergies to cats emanates from their skin. Two proteins, Fel dI and *cat albumin,* found in the sebaceous and anal glands, are spread on a cat's coat when she licks herself. Once dry, the proteins come off easily and are carried through the air and deposited throughout the environment. To keep you responding to your cat instead of reacting to her, try some of these suggestions.

• Restrict the areas in your home that your cat can access.

• Clean the cat areas thoroughly weekly.

- Wash your bedding weekly.

- Bathe your cat in distilled water monthly.

- Make sure you have your allergy shots, and take any medication your doctor advises.

- Purchase a high-efficiency particulate air (HEPA) filter to remove allergens from your home.

- Eliminate carpets, drapes, and upholtstered furniture from the bedroom to keep your pillows, mattress, and bedding allergen free. Treat carpet and upholstered furniture in other rooms with an anti-allergen dust spray.

- Use allergen-proof vacuum cleaner bags.

- Use a dust-free litter made from recycled paper.

Saying Good-bye

Face it—cats are often our best friends. They are there during the most quiet, peaceful parts of our day. They love us even when others may not, and they comfort and console us when we need it most. Because cats are such an important part of our lives, they leave an empty space when they pass away. If your cat companion has died, dealing with the grief that results is often difficult. Many people do not understand why a person may feel the loss of a pet as deeply as when a human loved one has died. In some circumstances, we may be left to deal with the loss alone and without human support and consolation. If you would like to talk to someone who understands how you feel when your cat dies, see the resources at the end of this chapter for the telephone numbers of pet loss support hotlines. Although nothing can replace a beloved animal, we can help keep the memories alive and be comforted by them in various ways.

- Keep a journal that describes the things that your cat did, as a way of remembering the good times you had.

- Create a photo album or photo montage of your cat.

- Have a local artist paint a portrait of your cat.

- If you are handy with crafts, needlepoint a picture of your cat with her birth and death dates.

- Place a stone with your cat's name in your garden.

- Hold a memorial service for your cat that includes family and friends.

- Plant a tree, bush, or flower in remembrance of your cat.

- Make a donation to your favorite animal charity in your cat's name. Inquire if they have special giving categories such as putting a cat's name on a shelter cage or onto a brick that becomes part of a new building.

- Gather up your cat's belongings and store them in a special container that you can retrieve when the pain heals.

- Place your cat's ashes in an urn to keep nearby.

- If you prefer to bury your cat in a cemetery, check local ones for those that have special pet burial locations. Or, contact your local humane organization or shelter to ask if they provide pet burial services.

- If you have Internet access, visit The Pet Loss Grief Support Website & Candle Ceremony at *Petloss.com* where you can have your cat's name listed.

- Contact your local humane society to see if they have a support group where people meet to share their experiences. Often, talking with other pet people who understand what we are going through helps us deal with the loss.

Seasonal Resources

For more information about airplane travel regulations, contact the United States Department of Agriculture's Animal and Plant Health Inspection Service automated information line at 800-545-USDA (8732) and follow the instructions.

Try one of these books to find pet-friendly boarding or things to do with your pet while on the road.

🐱 Weekes, Greg, "The AAA Petbook: The AAA Guide to More Than 10,000 Pet-Friendly, AAA Rated Lodgings Across the United States & Canada," American Automobile Association, 1999.

🐱 Fish, Robert, and Kathleen D. Fish, "Pets Welcome: A Guide to Hotels, Inns and Resorts That Welcome You and Your Pet," Bon Vivant Press, 1998.

🐱 For the wonderful adventures of a laid-back, traveling cat, read "The Cat Who Went to Paris" (1996) and "A Cat Abroad: The Further Adventures of Norton, the Cat Who Went to Paris, and His Human" (1994), both by Peter Gethers, available from Fawcett Books.

🐱 For information about trapping cats or obtaining a humane trap, contact Alley Cat Allies, 1801 Belmont Street, NW, Suite 201, Washington, DC, 20009-5164, 202-667-3630, or visit them on the Web at *www.alleycat.org/*

For locations of pet sitters near you, contact these organizations:

🐱 Pet Sitters International locator line: 1-800-268-SITS

🐱 National Association of Professional Pet Sitters locator line: 1-800-296-PETS

🐱 For help dealing with grief over the loss of your pet, contact one of these pet loss support lines. Some support lines are staffed by veterinary students. Most lines operate only during specified times but give you the option of leaving a message. Be aware that you will bear the costs for long-distance telephone calls. Return calls will be collect.

- Companion Animal Association of Arizona, 602-995-5885

- Cornell University College of Veterinary Medicine, 607-253-3922

- Ohio State University School of Veterinary Medicine, 614-292-1823

- Tufts University School of Veterinary Medicine, 508-839-7966

- University of California at Davis, 530-752-4200

- University of Florida at Gainesville, 352-392-4700, ext. 4080

- Virginia-Maryland Regional College of Veterinary Medicine, 540-231-8038

- Visit the Pet Loss Grief Support Web Site & Candle Ceremony at *http://Petloss.com/*

Visit the library or a bookstore for books about dealing with pet loss:

- Anderson, Moira K., "Coping with Sorrow on the Loss of Your Pet," Alpine Publications, 1996.

- Sife, Wallace, "The Loss of a Pet: New Revised and Expanded Edition," IDG Books, 1998.

Helpful Hints for Cats with Disabilities

Have you ever seen a blind cat toss and play with a catnip toy or a deaf cat come for her dinner when the can opener runs? To us, a cat that has lost limbs or the use of some of her senses may seem incapable of enjoying life, but appearances may be deceiving. When dealing with disabilities, animals have the advantage. Cats don't sit around and pine about what they can no longer do. Unless your cat is so ill or injured that she cannot function at all, she will adjust to her limitations.

Aging Cats

Aging is a natural process. It results in changes in your cat's metabolism, hormone balance, and sensory perception. A cat is considered a senior between the ages of 7 and 12. Your aging cat will sleep more and experience degeneration of her body systems and internal organs. Expect her to have less tolerance of extremes in heat or cold, to have decreased immunity to disease and infection, and to experience a decline in her metabolism. An older cat may lose her vision and hearing. Because the older cat is generally less active, she requires fewer calories. If you have children in the house, make certain that they understand that your cat is elderly and requires more careful and sensitive handling.

• Have your veterinarian run appropriate tests to detect any illness or degenerative condition early so your cat can be treated. Pay attention to any changes in your cat's habits, behavior, or appearance, and report them to your veterinarian.

• Learn the symptoms of some of the more common problems that afflict the older cat, such as diabetes, kidney and thyroid disease, and heart conditions. If you notice any symptoms, contact your veterinarian right away.

• Discuss with your veterinarian feeding your geriatric cat a diet formulated specifically for the needs of older animals.

• As your cat ages, look for signs of dental problems. Clean her teeth regularly, and have your veterinarian professionally clean them when necessary.

• Cats become more creatures of habit as they age. If you are planning any environmental changes, do so gradually and pay special attention to your cat's needs to minimize any stress she experiences.

• When you groom your geriatric cat, look for lumps and bumps under her skin.

• Engage your older cat in moderate play to maintain muscle tone, increase circulation, and aid digestion.

• Keep your cat indoors to keep her safe and help her live longer.

Arthritis or Stiffness

As our cats age, their joints can stiffen and arthritis can set in. Arthritis has no cure. However, some of these suggestions may help to alleviate your cat's arthritic pain and make performing everyday functions a lot easier.

• Keep your cat's weight at a normal level. Added weight will put more stress on bones, joints, and muscles.

- Do not give aspirin to your cat unless advised to do so by your veterinarian. Aspirin can be extremely toxic.

- Make a set of steps or use footstools to help your cat reach her destination, such as her favorite sleeping chair. If the steps are wooden, tack carpet to them to prevent her from slipping.

- Make a carpet-covered ramp any place where there are stairs or steps from one room to the next.

- Let your cat use an elevated food bowl to keep her from having to bend over to eat.

- As an alternative, place your cat's food bowls in a stacking in/out tray designed for the office to raise them off the floor. The modular design will help you find the perfect height.

- To prevent Kitty from having to step over a high-sided litter box, use an aluminum baking pan with sides 2 or 3 inches (5 or 8 cm) high.

- Cut an opening in the front of a plastic litter box so that Kitty has less difficulty stepping into it.

- Use a paint tray as a litter box. One side will be low so a sick or arthritic cat can step into it without pain.

Blindness or Vision Problems

As with most other physical limitations, your cat will adapt to loss of sight and learn to function by using her other senses. Occasionally, the loss occurs slowly as she ages rather than suddenly, giving her more time to adjust.

- Do not lift a blind cat. Because blind cats use spatial relationships to find their way around, lifting them causes disorientation and confusion when they are placed back down on the floor.

- Keep objects and furniture in the same spots because blind cats use their familiarity with their surroundings to find their way around. Rearranging the furniture confuses a blind cat and adds hazards to her environment.

- If your house is large, try restricting your blind cat to a small area so that she can learn her way around more quickly. Gradually allow her to have access to the rest of the house.

- If your cat has cataracts or low vision, keep a light turned on at night to help her see.

- If your cat's vision problems are due to cataracts, the cataracts can be removed surgically. Discuss options with your veterinarian.

- Construct a collar-mounted walking cane for your blind cat that curves forward and to the side to warn her of an impending object.

- Keep your blind cat's litter box in the same place. The last thing you want to do is move it to another location. Your blind cat just might decide to urinate where convenient.

Down the Hatch

Your cat's desire for food is determined as much by her sense of smell as it is by her sense of taste. When your cat comes down with a cold or flu that affects her ability to smell dinner, her appetite may not be what it normally is. If your cat is suffering from an illness, she may not want to eat. When she is sick, she needs nourishment the most, however. At those times, you may have to offer a helping hand to encourage your pet to devour dinner.

- Instead of shopping for her food in the cat food aisle of your grocery store, head for the shelves of baby food. Chicken-, turkey- or beef-flavored baby food will be more palatable, and the smooth texture will be easier to swallow and digest.

- Drain the liquid off of people tuna in water onto some of your cat's favorite dry food or onto a small amount of a bland-tasting canned cat food to whet your cat's appetite.

- If you have to force-feed your cat, mix a little of the baby food with water to make it a runny consistency. Give your cat eye droppers full of the mixture.

Hearing Problems

Deafness or hearing loss in cats may be due to genetic factors or the result of disease, injury, drug toxicity, or old age. Deaf cats can function just as normally as cats that can hear as long as you

HOW-TO: Provide Quality Home Care for the Sick Cat

When your pet is sick, caring for her in the comfort of her own home whenever possible will help reduce stress and will hasten recovery. If you would like to care for your cat at home rather than hospitalize her, discuss the options with your veterinarian. Make certain you know what is involved and that you can provide whatever care is necessary. If your cat requires shots, for example, be sure you are temperamentally suited to give them.

1. Discuss with your veterinarian any at-home treatment that must be administered to your cat, including medication, diet, exercise, or checkups.
2. If appropriate, set up a sick room for your cat with her bed, food, and litter box. If you detect that your cat would rather be with the members of the family, give her that option. A sick-room environment is beneficial to a cat only if she wants to be alone during recovery.
3. If you must administer medication, prepare a schedule for doing so or put the pill times on your daily planner or calendar.
4. Make sure your cat's bed is in a draft-free location. For extra warmth, add a blanket or flannel sheet, or use a heating pad or a hot-water bottle wrapped in a towel. A heat lamp may be used as an extra source of heat. However, be sure to keep it high above your cat's bed to prevent accidental burning.
5. Keep your recovering cat eating. Nourishment will speed the process.
6. If your cat cannot keep herself clean, wipe her with a sponge or cloth dampened with warm water. While your cat is ill, do not bathe her in water.
7. Provide plenty of fresh water for your convalescing cat. There are actually systems available today that filter and aerate your cat's water!
8. If your cat is recovering from surgery, use shredded newspaper or newspaper-type filler in her litter box rather than clay-type or clumping litter. Clay or clumping litter can stick to your cat's wound and cause it to become infected.

take a few precautions. To help your deaf cat manage, try some of these suggestions.

• Cats should not run loose. However, not allowing a cat to have free run is especially important when she can't hear the threat of danger, such as oncoming traffic.

• Make certain your cat sees you before you touch her. Touching a deaf cat before she is aware of your presence may cause her to react defensively.

• Use visual clues to get your deaf cat's attention. Hand signals can call your cat to your side when the sound of your voice will not.

• Try tapping on the floor with your fingers. The tapping will make slight vibrations that will get your deaf cat's attention.

• Instead of clicker training, use a flashlight flicked on and off to obedience train your cat.

• Alternatively, use thumbs-up and thumbs-down signals.

• Some deaf cats do pick up on high-pitched noises such as those emitted by dog whistles. Try using a dog whistle to call your deaf cat.

• To call your deaf cat to dinner or get her attention, flick lights on and off.

• Deaf cats that are a part of a multi-pet family often take their clues from the actions of other pets in the household. Your deaf cat may like to have a companion to help her along.

• Discuss with your veterinarian the option of obtaining a hearing aid for your cat. Hearing aids are not appropriate for all animals suffering hearing loss, but your cat may be a candidate if she has some hearing left.

Incontinence

Incontinence happens, to paraphrase the popular bumper sticker, and it may occur temporarily due to a bladder infection or permanently due to other illnesses or physical conditions. Before following any suggestion to deal with the incontinence, have your cat examined by a veterinarian to determine the source of the problem. If the incontinence is caused by an infection, it can be treated by antibiotics.

• Place pet pads that are plastic on one side and quilted on the other to absorb moisture or newspapers around the house so that your cat can get to them easily.

• Investigate using pet diapers on your incontinent cat. Pet diapers are used for females in heat.

• If your cat's incontinence was temporarily due to a bladder infection, you may have to retrain her to urinate in the litter box once the infection has cleared. See the chapter about behavior for training details and suggestions. Clean any urine spots with a good odor neutralizer so that your cat will not return to them the next time she must urinate.

Missing Limbs, Paralysis, Cerebellar Hypoplasia

Cats with missing limbs can adapt quite well to their situation, especially if they are given a little help from their owners. If your cat has lost a limb or the use of one or both, try some of these suggestions to help her get a leg up on her condition.

• Wheelchairs are available for pets with missing hind limbs, back problems, arthritis, paralysis, or other maladies. There are carts available in pet stores that keep your cat's hind legs off the ground so they bear no weight while she propels herself using her front legs.

• Carpeted ramps throughout the house will help a cat with ambulatory difficulties to get up onto furniture or move to any location that involves steps.

• Put your cat's bed on the floor in a draft-free spot to keep her from having to climb into bed.

• Use piles of pillows to ease your handicapped cat's transition to a higher location. The pillows will help her pull herself up and provide cushioning if she should fall.

• Use a litter box with one side completely open so that your cat can pull herself into the box. As an alternative, construct a carpeted ramp leading into the litter box.

Pill-Popping Time

Getting the pill into your cat can be frustrating when she seems to have other ideas about what she wants to put into her mouth. If your pet gives you flak at pill-popping time, try some of these tricks to maneuver the medicine into her mouth.

• Your veterinarian may be able to give you medicine for your cat in a variety of forms. Therefore, if you think administering liquid medicine, for example, will be easier, ask if what your veterinarian is prescribing comes in liquid form. Capsules seem to be the most difficult form of medicine to administer, so inquire as to whether the capsule contents can be removed and mixed with food.

• To administer liquid medicine, use a dosing syringe. Quickly squirt the medicine into your cat's mouth.

• A pill gun is a quick and effective way to give your pet a pill. They are available from veterinarians.

• Crush the pills, and mix with water. Give them to your cat in a syringe.

- If the medicine is a pill, roll a piece of cream cheese around it like a tiny meatball and watch your cat eat it without hassle.

- To make sure your cat gets the proper medication at the proper times, keep a calendar with the dates and times to administer the medication or list the times on your own personal day planner.

- To keep your cat from escaping while administering medication, position her between your legs with her head facing away from you as you kneel on the floor.

- If your cat squirms at pill-popping time, wrap her in a blanket or towel with only her head showing.

- Ask your veterinarian if the liquid medicine can be administered in food. If so, mix it with some liquid from people tuna packed in water or some clam juice.

- Break a pill into parts, and insert them into moist treats.

- Put the pill inside something your cat likes, such as a dab of mayonnaise, cottage cheese, yogurt, or other goody.

- Grind up the pill, and mix it with a dab of butter. Rub it onto your cat's hair where she will lick off the mixture.

Urine Samples

Your veterinarian may ask you to provide a sample of your cat's urine for analysis for sugar, blood, crystals, or other components. Depending on your cat, you may have to perform feats of acrobatics in order to catch a few drops as gravity pulls them from your cat into the litter box. If obtaining a urine sample has you mystified, place your cat's litter box with the litter in it inside a lightweight plastic trash bag. Tie the bag with a twist tie. Your cat will feel the litter under her feet and use the box, leaving a pool of urine in the middle of the bag. Scoop up the urine using a syringe or medicine dropper, and put it into a container with a lid.

Resources for Disabled Cats

Check out some of these books to help you care for your elderly or ill pet.

Bessant, Claire, and Bradley Viner, "The Ultrafit Older Cat," Barron's Educational Series, 1997.

Pinney, Roy, "Caring for Your Older Cat," Barron's Educational Series, Inc., 1996.

Thornton, Kim Campbell, and John Hamil, "Your Aging Cat: How to Keep Your Cat Physically and Mentally Healthy into Old Age," IDG Books, 1997.

Helpful Hints for Cat Owners with Disabilities

Everyone who has ever owned a cat knows how beneficial they can be. Cats provide us with love and companionship. They make us feel more relaxed and better equipped to handle the demands of daily life. Living with animals lowers blood pressure and reduces stress, even for those of us blessed with good health and complete functioning of our body parts. However, pets are especially important to people with physical limitations or disabilities. Caring for a cat may mean the difference between feeling isolated and feeling as though a friend is always close at hand. The other side of the coin, however, is that pets need care. Those of us who may benefit the most from having a companion cat are often less able to care for them. The following hints are designed to help people who suffer from any one of a variety of different physical constraints. Almost all of them came from other pet owners who have experienced the limitation in question. Many of the products discussed in this chapter are available in kitchen stores or adaptive tool catalogs.

Arthritis or Carpal Tunnel Syndrome

If you suffer from arthritis or any problems involving your hands, such as carpal tunnel syndrome, just opening a can of cat food can be a major ordeal. If you prepare your cat's food, cutting and cooking it may lessen the stress on your finger joints. The solution may be as simple as having the right tools for the right job.

• Many cat foods come in flip-top cans. Some can be difficult to pull open. To help get the lid off, use a device available in kitchen stores that resembles a small bottle opener to slide under the tab and gain extra leverage. If you cannot find such a device, simply open the can with a can opener as you would a can without a flip top, or flip it open with a bottle opener by inserting the opener under the tab.

• Electric can openers are easier to manipulate than hand can openers if your cat's food does not come in flip-top cans. Even if your cat's food does come in a flip-top can, you can open it with the electric can opener if you have trouble flipping its top.

• If you must raise your cat's can of food until you reach a level of comfort for opening it, sit one can on top of another. This is especially useful if you are feeding your pet the 5.5-ounce (156-g) size.

• Some of the tools available at kitchen or housewares stores have larger handles to make gripping easier.

• Kitchen tools with swivel handles assist you if your wrist rotation ability is limited so that you do not spill things off the spoon.

• If you have no strength in your hands, you can use adaptive silverware that can attach to your hands for scooping out your cat's dinner.

• A V-shaped jar opener that attaches to the underside of a cupboard enables you to slide a jar into it then turn the jar until the lid opens. This is useful for any cat product that comes in a jar with a lid or even for opening baby food if you must feed your cat baby food when she is ill.

• As an alternative, use a simple, round device made of rubber that you place on top of the jar lid to help you grip it when opening it.

• To help you open boxes of your cat's dry food, use a device with a built-up handle that you simply insert and lift.

• To groom your cat, attach to your cat's brush a universal cuff or wrist cuff designed to hold utensils for people with limited hand strength. Slip your hand into the cuff, and pull the brush over your cat.

Back Problems

As we age, flexibility may diminish and bending over becomes more difficult. Back surgery, degenerative spinal conditions, or even muscle spasms or temporary pain due to a variety of causes can prevent us from stooping over to pick up even the tiniest speck let alone a 50-pound (23-kg) bag of Kitty's cat box filler. Try some of these time-tested tips to help with tasks you need to do when your back puts a cramp in your style.

• To transport heavy containers of cat food or litter, use a child's wagon or a garbage can on wheels.

• Use a wheeled luggage cart strong enough to carry at least 50-pound (23-kg) bags of food or litter that is inexpensive and easily slipped into the trunk of your car. Wheeled luggage carts are available in the luggage sections of department stores and cost about $10.

• Ask your local grocery store if it offers delivery service or check the Yellow Pages of your telephone directory for commercial delivery services that would pick up your cat's food and litter for you.

• Order your cat's food and supplies from Web pet stores and have them delivered right to your door.

• Purchase a long-handled scoop to minimize bending when scooping the litter box or getting dry food out of a large bag and placing it in your cat's dish. Some long-handled scoops double as pet food bag clasps to keep the bag closed and prevent excess air from making your cat's food stale.

- To take your cat to the vet, use a wheeled pet carrier or a crate dolly.

- To groom your cat, have the pet come up to the table or countertop instead of you sliding down onto the floor.

- To scoop kitty wastes from the clumping litter, use a long-handled pooper scooper or rake. They come in a variety of styles with handles up to 36 inches (91 cm) long.

- As an alternative to using a carrier, try carrying your cat in a backpack or sling tote specially designed for carrying pets under 15 pounds (7 kg).

- To lift and lower your cat's food and water bowls, use a long-handled dustbin.

- To eliminate the need to refill your cat's water dish as often, try one of the bowls in which you insert an upside-down 2-liter soda bottle that you fill with water.

- Place your cat's food and water dishes on a wooden bench, table, or countertop. Your cat will have no trouble jumping up to feed from the bowls.

- Elevate your cat's litter box by placing it on a sturdy box or bench. Use a covered box to keep the litter from scattering onto the floor.

- Purchase an elevated litter box to avoid having to bend over to clean it.

- Use one of the newer, lightweight litters that are more absorbent yet easier to lift when wet from use.

HIV/AIDS

If you are a cat owner with HIV/AIDS, just cleaning up after your cat may require more effort than you can muster. Your suppressed immune system also makes you susceptible to secondary infections and illnesses. Zoonotic diseases—those that can be transmitted from animals to people—occur fairly uncommonly. In most cases, they are not life threatening. However, for the person with a suppressed immune system, zoonotic diseases may pose a special threat. If you have a cat, you have more of a risk of contracting toxoplasmosis or cat scratch fever, two diseases that can be transferred from cats to people. Toxoplasmosis is a parasitic infection with symptoms similar to the common cold. A single exposure normally ensures immunity to future exposure to the disease, but natural immunity may not develop in a person whose immune system is compromised. The two major sources of toxoplasmosis are raw or undercooked meat and the feces of cats. Research has shown, however, that people with HIV are more likely to be exposed to *Toxoplasma gondii*, the toxoplasmosis-causing pathogen, from ingesting undercooked meat than from contact with a cat's litter box. Cat scratch fever can cause lymph node enlargement, fever, fatigue, sore throat, and headaches. Infected cats show no signs of illness but carry the disease-causing pathogen on their claws or teeth.

Having to give up a beloved cat companion during a time when you need her most adds a dimension of suffering that could be prevented. Before you find another home for the cat you would rather keep with you, try some of these suggestions to help you provide continuing care.

• As part of your cat's annual checkup, have her stools checked by a veterinarian for parasites. Medicate your cat appropriately to eliminate them.

• Do not feed your cat raw or undercooked meats or unpasteurized milk.

• Practice good hygiene by keeping your surroundings clean. Use household bleach as a good germ killer, or purchase an antibacterial cleaning product to eliminate germs from where your cat sleeps or walks.

• Wear rubber gloves when cleaning up a cat mess. Avoid direct contact with your cat's bodily fluids such as vomit, feces, urine, or saliva. Wash your hands and the gloves after cleaning up.

• If you have been bitten, rinse the wound or scratch right away with a mild soap and water.

- Contact a local chapter of Pets Are Wonderful Support (PAWS) or Pets Are Loving Support (PALS) to request a volunteer to help you care for your pet. PAWS groups operate nationwide and are dedicated to keeping pets with their HIV/AIDS-affected owners. They can supply volunteers to lend a hand as well as information about keeping pets for the person who has been diagnosed with HIV. PAWS volunteers will clean the litter box, feed and water your cat, and provide other pet-related services. If no volunteers are available where you live, consider contacting a commercial service to help you care for your cat. Pet sitters often offer additional services at a fee to pet owners who are incapacitated, so check the Yellow Pages under "Pet Sitters."

- If you have no local PAWS chapter, contact your local AIDS resource center for advice on caring for your cat.

- Clean your cat's litter box daily. Because toxoplasmosis oocytes take at least 48 hours to shed, daily removal of feces prevents toxoplasmosis from becoming a threat.

- Keep your cat's nails trimmed or cap them with tips that fit over them to keep her from scratching her claws on you.

- Do not play games with your cat that involve the direct use of your hands.

- Cats can catch toxoplasmosis from eating rodents. To minimize the risk, keep your cat indoors or, if you allow your cat outside, put a bell on her collar to help warn potential prey of her presence.

- Instead of scooping out wastes from your cat's litter box, use disposable plastic liners and change them each time you change the litter.

Vision Limitations

Losing one's sight either permanently or temporarily or even having it decreased due to cataracts or other causes can cause you as a cat owner to rethink how to manage everyday care of your cat. Simply finding your cat in your home may represent an ordeal, much less being able to tell if she is sick or injured. The following are some tips for people with vision-related problems from people who have vision problems themselves. Some of the tips will help you if you have completely lost your vision, but others require you to be able to discern shapes or contrasts.

• To help know where your cat is, put a bell on her collar. If you have more than one cat, use different-sounding bells.

• As an alternative, put her rabies tag and metal license next to each other on her collar so they jingle when she walks.

• Telling your cats apart if you have more than one may be as simple as touching them and feeling their coats. To help differentiate between the two cats, put different types of collars on them. Use different combinations, such as a collar with a metal buckle and one with a plastic buckle or one collar made from elastic and the other one made from plastic to help you tell them apart.

• If your cat has a dark coat, place light-colored scatter rugs at the doors to the outside of your home so that you can see her against the light background when you enter or leave your house. This will prevent your cat from escaping accidentally. Conversely, if your cat has a light coat, place dark scatter rugs at your doors.

• If you have a neighbor, relative, or friend who does your grocery shopping for you, peel a label from your cat's food and give it to the shopper so that he or she buys the correct variety or brand.

• If you feed your cat more than one flavor of food, put a rubber band around the cans of one flavor and not the other to be able to tell by feeling for the presence of rubber bands which one you are feeding her.

• To measure quantities of food for your cat, keep the appropriately sized measuring cup in the bag of food so you will always feed the correct amount.

• Place a tray with 1/2-inch (1-cm) sides, such as a cookie sheet or pizza tray, along a wall where you are less likely to step on it accidentally. When you feed your cat, place her food and water on the tray to catch spills.

• Find someone in your vicinity who provides taxi service for your cat's veterinary trips. A pet sitter or pet care professional also may have such services. Check the Yellow Pages of your phone directory under "Pets" or "Pet Sitters." Inquire at local pet stores if none are listed in the telephone directory.

• Some veterinarians make house calls. If transportation is a problem for you, find a veterinarian that will come to your home.

• If you must give your cat medication, ask for it in pill form so that you don't have to measure dosages in a dropper as you would when using liquids.

• If the medicine comes in a capsule and must be divided, open the capsule and pour the white powder onto a dark tile or board for contrast. Divide the powder into parts with a knife. Sprinkle the portion over your cat's food, and mix it in.

• To tell if your cat is sick, pay attention to her activity level and touch her nose, ears, and foot pads. A dry nose, warm ears, and warm foot pads along with diminished activity may indicate that your cat is not feeling well.

• Line your cat's box with a litter liner. Simply remove it and the contents periodically, and throw away.

• Run a heavy-duty litter scoop back and forth through the litter. Judge by the weight of the scoop when to lift it up. Deposit wastes into a small, plastic trash can you keep next to the litter box.

• Use a plastic bag such as those in which newspapers are wrapped over your hands and search the box. This is especially useful if you think your cat has diarrhea. You will be able to tell from the feel of the feces if it is solid or loose.

• To prevent your cat from scattering litter around the box, use a covered box that keeps the litter contained.

Weakness

In some cases, degenerative conditions may cause us to become weak and unable to perform tasks that require a certain amount of strength. If caring for your cat has become difficult because of weakness, here are some suggestions for strengthening your physical resources. (You can also read the section "Back Problems" for more suggestions.)

• When your cat must visit the veterinarian, investigate mobile veterinarians who will come to your house. Mobile veterinarians are especially helpful if you have several pets. The mobile vet can check on all of the cats at one time. Check the Yellow Pages of your telephone directory under "Veterinarians" for listings.

• Many groomers operate mobile facilities and, like mobile veterinarians, will come to your home to conduct the necessary grooming. Check the Yellow Pages under "Grooming."

• If you need help giving your cat medicine, fluids, or shots, ask your veterinarian if he or she knows of anyone who will make home visits. If not, contact local pet sitters to find ones who will assist you. Many pet sitters are trained to perform these functions for the sick pet for owners who cannot perform them for themselves or for owners when they are away. Check the Yellow Pages under "Pet Sitters."

• When feeding and giving water to your cat, use large bowls so that you don't have to refill them as often.

• Ask a friend or relative to divide your cat's food into smaller containers you can lift more easily.

• To play with your cat, use flashlights or laser pointers. Cats will love chasing the light around and you will not have to make a move.

• Keep litter supplies, such as bags and scoops, near each litter location to minimize walking.

• Use clumping litter to prevent discarding good litter and washing litter boxes too frequently.

• If you are considering bringing a cat into your home, opt for an older, more quiescent cat rather than a kitten that you may trip over or use all of your energy when chasing her around the house.

• Instead of adopting a cat, give one a test-drive by fostering for a local shelter or animal organization. Shelters need good homes for cats that come to them. Many shelters have foster programs that provide temporary homes for cats and kittens until permanent ones can be found.

Wheelchair Bound

Being confined to a wheelchair poses a whole set of problems when caring for a cat. Because we are constantly seated, everything that is either above or below arm's length is simply out of reach. Try some of these suggestions for getting a grip on caring for your cat.

• A long-handled device that looks like a tong and has a jaw on one end was designed to help people reach and grab items out of their grasp. While useful when grocery shopping, the arm-extending device is also useful at home to grab your cat's food from the cupboard or countertop.

• Extend your reach with long-handled kitchen tools, commonly used for barbecuing. Tongs and sturdy spatulas allow you to pick up and lower your cat's food and water dishes. Long-handled kitchen tools are available in hardware, kitchen, and department stores.

• As an alternative, use a long-handled dustbin to raise and lower your cat's food dishes from and to the floor.

• To have water available for your cat when you need it, have someone fill plastic gallon (liter) jugs with water and put them on the floor near your cat's water dish. This makes filling the bowls easier when seated.

- Put your cat's canned food into a soda chute designed to hold cans of soda in the refrigerator. If placed in the cupboard, the soda chute will dispense cans of cat food and keep you from having to reach to the back of the cupboard for them.

- If getting to the veterinarian is difficult, find a mobile veterinary clinic that will come to your home.

- Try making this homemade cat food bowl. Cut an opening large enough for your cat to eat from but not so large that the bottle loses its shape in the front of a gallon-sized (4 L-sized) plastic milk or water bottle. Place your cat's food in the bottom of the plastic bottle. Raise or lower it by grabbing the container by hand or with a reacher. The plastic milk bottle is very lightweight. Even with cat food in it, it is still not that heavy to lift.

- Place your cat's food dishes on a table or stool that is easy for you to reach and your cat to climb onto.

- Great cat toys for owners who must remain seated or relatively stationary are ones that are connected to a 3-foot (1-m) cord or fishing line that is attached to a long, flexible pole. The toys have about 6 feet (2 m) of reach, and using one is a great way to get your cat to exercise when you cannot.

Resources for People with Physical Limitations

If you suffer from HIV/AIDS, visit the San Francisco PAWS web page for a listing of chapters nationwide at *www.pawssf.org/chapters.html*

The following are two vendors of assistance devices for the elderly and disabled.

Assistive Devices, Inc., in Austin, TX, 800-856-0889 or *http://www.geocel.com/adi/*

CARE4U—Aids for Daily Living at *www.care4u.com/*

Pet Supply Sources

Internet Pet Stores

Pet supply stores on the Internet will deliver food, toys, litter, and other cat supplies to your door.

Amazon.com for cat books: *www.amazon.com*
Pet Planet: *www.petplanet.com*
Petopia: *www.petopia.com*
The Pet Channel: *www.thepetchannel.com*
The Pet Store: *www.petstore.com*

Pet Supply Catalogs

If you would like to mail order pet products, try perusing these pet supply catalogs.

Cat Claws, Inc.
P.O. Box 1774
Des Plaines, IL 60018
www.catclaws.com

Cats, Cats, and More Cats
2 Greycourt Avenue
P.O. Box 560
Chester, NY 10918
914-782-4141
marketplaza.com/cats/cats.html

Direct Book Service
P.O. Box 1778
701B Poplar
Wenatchee, WA 98807-2778
1-800-776-2665 to request a catalog
http://205.243.62.12/directbook/

The Humane Catalog
The Humane Society of the United States
P.O. Box 1519
Elmira, NY 14902-1723
www.hsus.org

That Pet Place
237 Centerville Road
Lancaster, PA 17603
1-800-THAT PET
www.thatpetplace.com

Index